*Pressure Groups, Politics and
Democracy in Britain*

CONTEMPORARY POLITICAL STUDIES SERIES

Series Editor: John Benyon, *University of Leicester*

A series which provides authoritative and concise introductory accounts of key topics in contemporary political studies

Other titles in the series include:

Elections and Voting Behaviour in Britain
DAVID DENVER, *University of Lancaster*

Political Parties in the UK Since 1945
Edited by ANTHONY SELDON, *Institute of Contemporary British History*

The Constitution in Question
Edited by JOHN BENYON, *University of Leicester*

CONTEMPORARY POLITICAL STUDIES

# Pressure Groups, Politics and Democracy in Britain

WYN GRANT

*University of Warwick*

Philip Allan

NEW YORK  LONDON  TORONTO  SYDNEY  TOKYO

First published 1989 by
Philip Allan
66 Wood Lane End, Hemel Hempstead
Hertfordshire, HP2 4RG
A division of
Simon & Schuster International Group

Printed and bound in Great Britain by
Billing and Sons Ltd, Worcester

British Library Cataloguing in Publication Data

Grant, Wyn, 1947—
    Pressure groups, politics and democracy in Britain. —
    (Contemporary political studies)
    1. Great Britain. Politics. Role of pressure groups
    I. Title  II. Series
    322.4′3′0941
    ISBN 0-86003-415-1
    ISBN 0-86003-715-0 (pbk)

2  3  4  5   93  92  91

# Contents

Preface   vii

**1 Introduction: The Key Characteristics of Pressure Groups**   **1**
What is a pressure group?   3
Social movements   5
Quasi-governmental organisations   6
Political parties   8
A working definition of a pressure group   9
Typologies of groups   11
Pressure groups and democracy   21

**2 Pressure Groups and the Political System**   **24**
Pluralism   25
Policy communities   30
Corporatism   32
The liberal critique of pressure groups   36
The Tory defence of interest   42
Socialist views of pressure groups   43
Technostructure   44

**3 How Pressure Groups Influence Whitehall and the Political Agenda**   **47**
Getting issues on the political agenda   48
Food additives: a case study of issue emergence   51
Influencing the executive branch of government   55
Policy implementation and enforcement   63

**4  Exerting Pressure Outside Whitehall**                        **67**
   Parliament                                                   67
   Pressure groups and the party system                         76
   Pressure groups and the media                                79
   Pressure groups and the courts                               84
   Local government                                             85

**5  Pressure Groups and the European Community**                **90**
   Influencing the Community through the national government     94
   European-level pressure groups                               98
   Direct contacts with Community institutions                 107
   Conclusions                                                 111

**6  The Effectiveness of Pressure Groups**                     **113**
   Why measuring pressure group influence is difficult         114
   A typology of factors affecting pressure group effectiveness 117
   Conclusions                                                 131

**7  Groups in Action: A Case Study of Agriculture
   and the Environment**                                       **133**
   The success of the agricultural lobby                       134
   Forestry: a closed policy community                         140
   Is the farming lobby losing ground?                         145
   Agriculture and the environment                             148

**8  Conclusions: Pressure Groups and Democracy**               **152**
   Thatcherism and pressure group activity                     152
   The case for pressure groups reviewed                       155
   The limits to pressure group power                          163

   References                                                  165
   Index                                                       172

# Preface

This book seeks to provide a general introduction to the role of pressure groups in British democracy for those relatively unfamiliar with the subject. Readers who wish to follow up the subject in more depth by reading some of the academic literature on pressure groups can refer to the list of references at the end of the book.

As well as making use of what is now an extensive literature on pressure groups, this book draws on interviews I have conducted over the years with pressure group officials, politicians and civil servants. Some of this research has been funded by the Economic and Social Research Council and by the Nuffield Foundation.

I would like to express my appreciation to the series editor, John Benyon, for suggesting that I should write this book and for his helpful comments on the first draft. Samuel Brittan, assistant editor of the *Financial Times*, and honorary professor of politics at Warwick University, commented on one section of the manuscript. As always, thanks are due to my wife, Maggie, for her support.

This book is dedicated to the memory of my uncle, Sidney Field, who sadly died before publication. Conversations I heard as a child in his newsagents shop in Plumstead SE18 helped to stimulate my interest in politics, and gave me my first lessons in looking for the 'story behind the story' in the day's newspapers.

Wyn Grant
Leamington Spa

# 1

# Introduction: The Key Characteristics of Pressure Groups

Every four years or so the majority of British electors go to schools, village halls, and a variety of other polling stations throughout the country to cast their votes in a general election. In between the four-year intervals, a minority of voters exercise their right to vote in local and European elections. For most electors, voting is their main point of contact with the democratic process. Only a small and declining minority are members of political parties. More people are members of the Royal Society for the Protection of Birds than of the Labour Party.

Every day, the paid officials and members of pressure groups are engaged in a wide variety of activities designed to influence the course of government policy. On a typical working day in London, there will be thousands of personal or telephone contacts between pressure group officials and civil servants. For example, it is likely that CBI officials will travel from their offices at Centre Point to meet civil servants at the Treasury or the offices of the Department of Trade and Industry in Victoria Street. Officials of the National Farmers' Union will most likely be travelling across the capital from their headquarters in Knightsbridge to a meeting at the Ministry of Agriculture, Fisheries and Food just off Whitehall. In the lift, they might meet officials from the Food and Drink Federation who have made the short journey from their headquarters near Aldwych. Some of these contacts will be concerned with European Community proposals, and in Brussels, equally, officials of the European organisations representing a variety of interests will be travelling to the

1

Commission's Berlaymont building or to its other offices scattered round the city.

Although many of the meetings taking place will be between pressure group officials and their counterparts in the civil service, many other types of contact will be taking place. A junior minister at the Department of Health may be meeting a delegation of junior hospital doctors concerned about their working hours. In Parliament, lobbyists for the disabled may be shepherding a group of people with a particular disability towards a sympathetic group of MPs with whom to talk about the limitations of the provisions made by government to deal with their special needs.

Some of the activities taking place will be less orthodox in character, and are sometimes referred to as 'protest group' activities. The police may have to be called to a town hall when protesters opposing a proposed development get out of hand in the public gallery. Members of Greenpeace may be attempting to board a ship in the North Sea which is burning off poisonous wastes. Animal rights activists may be breaking into a research laboratory to rescue animals. The Campaign for Nuclear Disarmament (CND) grew rapidly in the early 1980s into a movement of a quarter of a million members. Public rallies were supplemented by direct action tactics by groups associated with CND, although organisationally distinct from it, such as the women's peace camps at Greenham Common (see Byrd 1988).

Clearly, pressure group activity represents an important part of the political process in Britain; certainly, more citizens are involved in pressure group activity than in political parties. The 1970s and 1980s have seen a proliferation of 'cause' groups, particularly those concerned with environmental issues, ranging from global pollution problems to the protection of a particular species of animal. Groups representing 'sectional' interests, such as the British Medical Association or the Chemical Industries Association, continue to play a significant role in the political process. Business alone is represented by over 1,800 associations.

Much of this book will be concerned with explaining how pressure groups set about seeking to influence political decisions. How are they organised, and what kinds of strategies and tactics do they use? However, an attempt will also be made to tackle broader issues about the role of pressure groups in a democracy. Does the existence of such groups enhance the democratic process, or undermine it? Do the activities of pressure groups tend to reinforce existing distributions of power in society, or can they bring about fundamental changes? Before starting to answer these questions, it is necessary to explore what is meant by a 'pressure group'. A number of problems have to be resolved before a definition can be attempted.

## What is a pressure group?

This book is concerned with groups that seek to influence public policy — which can be formulated by central government, local government, the European Community, or, in some cases, by quasi-governmental organisations. The emphasis on public policy is important because any organised entity with the capacity to make authoritative decisions may develop internal pressure groups. For example, a firm may be viewed as a political organisation, and groups within it may lobby for a particular investment decision. In the case of a firm, such groups will not normally be formally constituted, but their identity will often be well known to other participants in a decision-making process. Other groups with decision-making authority may see the formation of advocacy groups with a particular purpose: for example, the movement for the ordination of women within the Church of England, or the group of members of the Abbey National Building Society fighting to prevent its conversion into a company. Groups of this kind have their own fascination, but the focus of this book is on the political processes of society as a whole, rather than on particular organisations within it, however significant they may be either to their own members or to society in general.

This book is concerned with organised entities that have such characteristics as a defined membership, stated objectives in relation to public policy and, often, a paid staff working to attain those objectives. Focusing on such groups raises four difficult problems of exclusion through the use of a particular definition of a pressure group: the relationship between an 'interest' and the pressure groups that seek to promote it; the relationship between a 'social movement' and the pressure groups it generates; the problem of pressure exerted by a single actor such as a firm; and the problem of whether parts of the machinery of government itself can be regarded as pressure groups.

The first of these problems, then, is concerned with the relationship between an 'interest' and the groups that represent that interest. 'Interest' is a word with many meanings. Some of these, such as a legal concern or pecuniary stake in property, or the payment of money to service a debt, need not be discussed here. Other meanings, such as the idea of the selfish pursuit of one's own welfare, have value-laden overtones which are best avoided. The meaning of interest which is particularly relevant here is what the *Concise Oxford Dictionary* terms a 'thing in which one is concerned; principle in which a party is concerned; party having a common interest (*the brewing interest*). So defined, interest covers both the pursuit of causes (such as prison reform) and the promotion and defence of particular stakes in the economy (such as those of farmers).

However, 'interest' has been especially used to apply to particular economic identities. Not all of these identities have been organised, at least not as a whole. For example, it has been common to speak of the 'City interest'. This has been considered a very influential interest in Britain for a long time. The influence of the City is often blamed for the overvaluation of sterling for long periods of modern British history, an overvaluation which damaged the international price competitiveness of British manufacturing industry. However, the influence of the City did not rest on its possession of well organised interest groups. The traditional channel for conveying 'City opinion' to the government was through the Governor of the Bank of England. Very often, however, the influence of the City did not require any overt expression of view. Treasury officials and the City shared common, unquestioned assumptions about the need to maintain the value of sterling. Any sign of pressure on sterling as a result of a loss of confidence in the financial markets was often enough to persuade governments to change their economic policies.

Unorganised interests are, however, tending to diminish in significance. In the City, trade associations for various financial interests, formerly of little significance, have assumed a new importance. There are a variety of reasons for this particular change in the City, including a decline in its social cohesion, the removal of traditional barriers between different types of financial institution, and a new regulatory regime which has transformed the role of many trade associations. That is not to say that the Chancellor no longer sounds out 'City opinion' at informal lunches, or that governments do not anxiously watch trends in 'market sentiment'. Even so, the exercise of influence in modern conditions requires organisation. The study of pressure groups is the study of *organised* interests, although one must always be aware that behind well-defined organisations lurk more amorphous but nevertheless significant 'bodies of opinion'.

## Social movements

The discussion so far has focused on 'sectional' economic interests rather than 'causes', but problems can also arise in exploring the relationship between broad social movements, and the pressure groups that spring from those movements. Consider one of the most important social movements of the late twentieth century: feminism. Women who consider themselves feminists hold a variety of views, and reflect those views in a variety of ways in their life style. They would probably, however, agree that they are concerned with redefining the role, and reasserting the status, of women in a society which has previously been dominated by the assumptions and preferences of men.

The required changes can be brought about in a number of ways. For many women, the most important change would be a mental one: thinking about the world in terms of feminist principles and arguments. This change of perception would affect the conduct of a woman's everyday life in terms of her relations with men and with other women; her relations with her family; and her career objectives and behaviour in the workplace. Many important changes can be sparked off by individual women reading feminist literature, or watching television programmes with a feminist perspective, or discussing their reading and viewing informally with other women. It is possible for a woman to regard herself as part of the 'feminist movement' without belonging to any organisation or even an informal mutual help group.

Even so, it is clear that many of the goals of the women's movement require political action if they are to be achieved. For example, better day-care facilities are necessary if women, particularly less well-off women, are not to be prevented from pursuing their careers. The feminist movement may have drawn attention to the serious problem of domestic violence, but political action is necessary if the police are to be persuaded to regard violence by a husband against his wife as a criminal offence; and funds are necessary to provide counselling, refuge and general assistance to battered wives. (For a discussion of women's aid, see Stedward 1987.) Thus there is here a broad social movement of which pressure group activity forms only one part. Indeed, women's aid groups have stressed such values as complete participation, the authenticity of personal experience, and collective self-organisation (Stedward 1987, p. 232). When pressure group activity springs from a social movement, it may thus reflect the characteristics of that movement (although, clearly, individuals subscribing to a broad goal — such as the abolition of hunting

— may differ about how that goal should be achieved: a point to which we will return later in the book).

Another problem is the question of political pressure exerted by individual political actors, most importantly firms. It is clear that during the 1970s and 1980s in Britain there was a proliferation of direct political activity by firms, operating either through their own government relations divisions, or through paid lobbyists acting on their behalf (see Grant 1987). It would seem wrong to exclude this type of activity because it does not involve an organisation with a constitution, membership and paid officials. Jordan and Richardson (1987, pp. 14–18) are surely correct when they argue for a broad definition of 'pressure group' that accepts companies and corporations as groups. After all, such an approach meets the *Concise Oxford Dictionary's* definition of a 'group' as a 'number of persons or things standing close together'.

But then, how wide does one cast the net? For example, should government ministries be treated as pressure groups? After all, the Ministry of Agriculture, Fisheries and Food has often been portrayed as the 'client' of agricultural interests, whilst the Department of Trade and Industry has often been regarded as close to business interests. This could seem to be stretching the term too widely. Ministries do, of course, often fight for the 'departmental view' within Whitehall, and that view often reflects to some extent the perspective and priorities of the pressure groups within the ministry's orbit (a phenomenon that will be explored more fully in Chapter 2 when 'policy communities' are discussed). However, ministries always have to aggregate the views of their client groups, rather than simply acting as their representatives within the government machine. 'Aggregation' often involves reconciling the divergent views of different groups; it will certainly involve placing their views within the context of both the policy of their own minister and of the government as a whole.

## Quasi-governmental organisations

Quasi-governmental organisations such as the Countryside Commission or the Equal Opportunities Commission pose more difficult problems. Such organisations have a variety of functions:

1. *They may have a statutorily defined responsibility for offering advice to the minister concerned on a particular policy area* as,

for instance, race relations. In other words, their formal responsibilities may require them to act as a pressure group for a particular cause.

2. *They may in practice be set up to act as a 'buffer' between the government and particular pressure groups.* Pressure groups can be deflected to the quasi-governmental body and thus kept at arm's length from government and away from busy ministers. Ministers faced with an awkward parliamentary question about a difficult political problem can claim that it is being reviewed by the relevant quasi-governmental body.

3. *Some quasi governmental bodies have been given the explicit or implicit task of mediating between rival groups.* For example, one of the more obscure quasi-governmental organisations, the Red Deer Commission, has as one of its tasks the resolution of conflicts between sporting interests wishing to have a sufficient number of deer to shoot at, and farmers annoyed by the damage done by marauding deer to their crops.

4. *Quasi-governmental bodies may be required to implement particular government policies or programmes.* However, as will be discussed later in the book, pressure groups are often given such responsibilities as well as part of their symbiotic relationship with government.

Quasi-governmental bodies perform a complex range of functions simultaneously, which may include pressure group activities. Consider, for example, the (English and Welsh) Milk Marketing Board. It has a *regulatory* function, in so far as it is responsible for implementing a statutorily-based milk marketing scheme which gives it disciplinary powers over farmers. It is involved in the *commercial* acquisition and disposal of milk. It is concerned with *promoting* milk as a product. It also has a clear *representative* function, both in relation to commercial dairy processors in a negotiating body known as the Joint Committee, and in discussions with the Ministry of Agriculture. It is in turn a member of the Federation of Milk Marketing Boards which is affiliated to the Dairy Trade Federation, so that it can also belong to a European Community-level organisation. Quasi-governmental organisations can act as pressure groups; they can belong to pressure groups; and they can mediate between pressure groups, or between pressure groups and the government. The range of their tasks draws attention to the fact that pressure groups function within a complex system of relationships which link a variety of political institutions and bodies. One sometimes has to look at pressure groups in isolation in order to understand their internal political and organisational dynamics, but one must also relate them to the broader political context in which they operate.

## Political parties

Political parties belong to that broader political context. Pressure groups may exist within political parties, as, for example, the Socialist Educational Association or the Socialist Medical Association within the Labour Party, or the Conservative branch of the Campaign for Homosexual Equality. However, I would argue for a clear distinction between pressure groups and political parties. Political parties seek to win seats in elections either with the objective of forming the government or part of the government (the most usual objective) or to acquire sufficient seats to bring about changes in the present constitutional arrangements of the country (a definition which could cover the Scottish and Welsh Nationalists and the various parties from Northern Ireland).

The range of concerns of political parties is typically wider than that of pressure groups. To be regarded as serious, they have to have policies which cover every conceivable issue of public interest (leaving aside those moral issues which are seen as a matter for personal judgement by individual MPs). The narrower concerns of pressure groups − with particular issues or interests − do not generally make contesting elections a viable strategy. Admittedly, they may do so to draw attention to the level of public concern on a particular issue (such as capital punishment) or to draw sufficient votes away from a particular party so as to make it lose a seat (the Conservatives lost the 1962 by-election in South Dorset to Labour because of the intervention of an anti-common market candidate who took 12.3 per cent of the vote, much more than the winning margin).

Pressure groups may, then, occasionally contest elections as a political tactic, although it is not a very effective one, and is mainly a sign of being outside the political mainstream. Sponsoring particular candidates selected by a political party, as some trade unions do in the Labour Party, is another matter, although again the political gains for the sponsoring body are questionable. In general, however, the distinction between a political party and a pressure group is a clear one. For example, at a number of points in the history of farmer representation in Britain, the possibility of organising a separate farmers' party has been discussed. The National Farmers' Union 'generally regarded a separate agricultural party as impracticable and over-ambitious — as indeed it was' (Self and Storing 1962, p. 44). (Agrarian parties have flourished in Scandinavian countries with proportional representation, but have become part of larger groupings as the agrarian share of the electorate has declined.) Farmers decided to take the pressure group route to pursue their interests.

## A working definition of a pressure group

We have dealt with the problems surrounding the definition of a pressure group; it is now possible to offer a working definition:

> A pressure group is an organisation which seeks as one of its functions to influence the formulation and implementation of public policy, public policy representing a set of authoritative decisions taken by the executive, the legislature, and the judiciary, and by local government and the European Community.

This definition includes 'think tanks' such as the Institute of Economic Affairs (IEA) as pressure groups, even though they do not engage in what would conventionally be regarded as lobbying. They do, however, seek to change the intellectual climate of opinion, which in turn influences the policy agenda and options available to ministers. It is generally agreed, for example, that bodies such as the IEA played an important role in paving the way for Thatcherism.

### Primary groups and secondary groups

The basic definition may be elaborated by making a distinction between primary and secondary pressure groups. Relatively few pressure groups are concerned simply with the representation of the interests or views of their members. (Examples are the Federation of Milk Marketing Boards and the former Food and Drink Industries Council.) Most groups offer services to members as a means of attracting and retaining their membership. In the case of an employers' organisation, this may be a sophisticated range of services from advice on the effective use of computers to representation before industrial tribunals. Groups pursuing particular causes usually provide their members with at least a magazine, and perhaps sell various goods to raise funds on which members are given a discount. A distinction may be made, however, between those organisations where the service function (either to members or to others) predominates, and those where services are provided as a membership incentive in order to recruit as large a portion as possible of the eligible membership. In the first category are members of the Automobile Association who see its primary function as the provision of a breakdown service, although the Association also lobbies government on transport policy questions. The Cats Protection League exists primarily to provide a rescue and rehabilitation service for abandoned and unwanted cats.

The dinstinction between primary and secondary pressure groups is not just one between the predominance of service provision compared with political representation in the organisation's work. There is a more general distinction between those organisations whose primary purpose is political, and those whose objectives lead them into political action from time to time. In some cases, this may mean that a particular part of the organisation has a special responsibility for political work. Consider the case of the Church of England. Its main purpose is that of a religious organisation: to provide facilities (buildings and clergy) for worship and the administration of the sacrament in accordance with its doctrinal beliefs, and to propagate its interpretation of the Christian gospel. However, it acts both as a 'sectional' pressure group in relation to its own particular interests and as a 'cause' group on wider social issues. In relation to its own material and institutional interests:

> ministers and/or MPs may be lobbied in order to influence tax or other measures affecting the institution as employer or property owner: examples are continuing attempts to gain exemption from Value Added Tax on repairs to church fabric; efforts to get favourable treatment under the terms of the Land Bill . . . and, in 1987, efforts to recoup possible losses flowing from the proposed abolition of rates and their replacement by a community charge.
>
> (Medhurst and Moyser 1988, p. 313)

The Church also comments on broad social and political issues (although some politicians would prefer it to concentrate on redeeming the souls of its members rather than intervening in broader moral questions). In practice, much of this work devolves on specialist boards of the General Synod. The Board for Mission and Unity finds itself involved in issues relating to the Third World and to South Africa. The Board of Education has a more difficult task: 'Whereas the Board may be perceived by the [Department of Education and Science] as a "peak association", able to negotiate authoritatively on behalf of Anglicans, those in Church House have in reality no real executive power vis-à-vis their constituents' (Medhurst and Moyser 1988, p. 329). The Board for Social Responsibility is perhaps the most politicised board, in part because 'its thinking on social policy is currently running counter to prevailing political orthodoxies' (p. 338). The prime purpose of the Church of England is, then, a religious one, but it has a secondary function as a pressure group seeking to influence public policy (albeit a rather special pressure group because of its status as an Established Church and the presence of bishops in the House of Lords).

Charities offer another interesting example. Their primary purpose is to collect funds in the pursuit of a defined charitable objective. They are unavoidably drawn into the political process because they are asked by government to offer advice on special policy areas (such as the welfare of a particular category of disabled person); or because they act as agents for the dispensation of government funds (for example, Third World aid is increasingly dispensed through charities). Charity law prevents them from engaging in overtly political activity. They do, however, need to engage in such activity from time to time because, for example, changes in tax law can have a significant impact on their ability to raise and retain funds. Thus medical research charities have formed an Association of Medical Research Charities which is able to pursue public policy issues on behalf of its members. This is a clear example of a primary pressure group.

It is apparent from the discussion so far that there are many different types of pressure group. Writers on pressure groups have attempted to categorise the main characteristics of pressure groups through a variety of typologies. The next section presents an evaluation of the main alternative typologies.

## Typologies of groups

A count of primary and secondary pressure groups in Britain which included locally based groups would almost certainly run into the tens of thousands (the Devlin Commission on industrial representation counted 1,800 business associations, which is only one of a number of categories). It is clearly not possible to study all these groups as individual organisations. Hence, a feature of the pressure group literature over the last thirty years has been a variety of attempts to create typologies to classify groups, not only for descriptive purposes, but also in the hope that such typologies might lead to useful generalisations about their behaviour.

One of the most important distinctions has been that between 'sectional' and 'cause' groups. Sectional groups 'represent a section of the community . . . Their function is to look after the common interests of that section and their membership is normally restricted to that section.' Cause groups 'represent some belief or principle . . . They seek to act in the interests of that cause. Theoretically their membership is not restricted at all. Anyone can join and by doing so signify his acceptance of the belief or principle' (Stewart 1958, p. 25). Sectional groups usually seek to organise as large a proportion of their eligible membership as possible. Their standing with government depends to a considerable extent on the validity of their claim to speak for a particular industry, group of employers or profession. Cause groups subdivide into those which seek a mass membership to take part in campaigning and those which seem content with a restricted membership, the implicit emphasis perhaps being on quality rather than quantity.

In general, most groups can be divided into the sectional or cause categories, although some cause groups may contain sectional interests within them. Kimber and Richardson (1974, p. 3) note that the Noise Abatement Society included manufacturers of noise suppression equipment among its members. Some local amenity groups may, whilst claiming to protect the environment in the interests of all, also have the effect, whether intended or not, of protecting the value of the property owned by existing residents. In their study of the Henley Society, Lowe and Goyder (1983, p. 121) note that 'Though the Society expresses the need for more low-cost accommodation in planning terms, it fails to make the link between the shortage of such accommodation and its own support for a strict policy of containment.' The planning policies it supports, mediated through market forces, 'increase the social exclusiveness of Henley' (p. 122). Indeed, the Society's support for more council housing 'may have been for reasons of self-interest, out of concern at the lack of service workers, rather than concern for those in housing need' (p. 123).

What useful generalisations does the sectional/cause distinction produce? First, it can be argued that the nature of the demands made by the two groups often tends to differ. Sectional groups are more likely to advance limited, specific goals which, as they are broadly coincident with the values of society as a whole, can be conceded without public controversy (see Jordan and Richardson 1987, p. 21). Sectional groups are often dealing with highly technical issues which do not interest the public at large, or which they would not understand. This does not mean that the resolution of the issue is unimportant to the members of the group concerned: it may have a considerable bearing on the profitability of an industry, or the future of a profession, but usually it will not become the subject of a wider public debate. 'On the contrary, a high-profile area such as nuclear policy or abortion or constitutional reform is unlikely to be resolved without wide participation and parliamentary legitimation' (p. 21).

Cause groups often have fewer resources at their disposal than sectional groups in terms of income and paid staff. Membership can be quite large: several of the environmental groups surveyed by Lowe and Goyder (1983) had a membership of over 100,000; and the Royal Society for the Protection of Birds had over 300,000 (561,000 by 1987). Greenpeace has 143,000 members in the UK and an annual turnover of £3 million. (The international membership is 2.5 million, with a turnover of £45 million.) The expansion of membership in the 1970s allowed environmental groups to take on more staff (see Table 1.1).

Although most cause groups have a much smaller membership, the drawbacks of a scruffy office and a poorly paid staff can to some extent be offset by their commitment to the cause, backed up by the willingness of members to work for the organisation free of charge. Thus, for example, in Amnesty International, 'The member is expected not just to contribute funds but also to work consistently both individually and in a group' (Ennals 1982, p. 68). Cause groups may also be able to win

**Table 1.1** Growth in staff numbers of selected environmental groups in the 1970s

|  | 1970 | 1979/80 |
|---|---|---|
| British Trust for Conservation Volunteers | 1 | 34 |
| Conservation Society | 0 | 2.5 |
| Council for Environmental Conservation | 0 | 5 |
| Council for Environmental Education | 1.5 | 4 |
| CPRE | 6 | 13 |
| Friends of the Earth | 1 | 21 |
| Keep Britain Tidy Group | 4 | 24 |
| National Society for Clean Air | 12 | 7 |
| Town and Country Planning Assoc. | 7 | 17 |
| Tree Council | – | 4 |
| Total | 32.5 | 131.5 |

*Source*: Adapted from Lowe and Goyder (1983, p. 48).

sympathetic attention from the media, and to mobilise public opinion. Even so, it may be difficult to sustain enthusiasm, and the ability of a sectional group to engage in long-drawn-out negotiations with the civil service may enable it to secure important concessions through a 'drip, drip, drip' process. There are, of course, plenty of sectional groups that have limited resources, but then they also have very limited aims.

It could be argued that sectional groups find it easier to recruit members because they appeal to a well-defined constituency with a particular interest at stake. (For a further discussion of this point in terms of Olsonian theory, see Chapter 2.) However, it has to be borne in mind that there has been a long-term trend for the membership of cause groups to rise (at the same time as political party membership has been declining). For example, following an expansion in the number of environmental groups in the late 1950s and early 1960s, there was a rapid expansion in their membership from the early 1970s onwards (Lowe and Goyder 1983, p. 17). (See Table 1.2.)

**Table 1.2** The growing membership of some leading environmental organisations (membership figures in thousands)

|  | 1971 | 1987 |
| --- | --- | --- |
| Amenity societies affiliated to the Civic Trust | 214 | 240 |
| Council for the Protection of Rural England | 21 | 32 |
| Friends of the Earth (England and Wales) | 1 | 55 |
| Ramblers Association | 22 | 57 |
| Royal Society for Nature Conservation | 64 | 184 |
| Royal Society for the Protection of Birds | 98 | 561 |
| World Wide Fund for Nature | 12 | 124 |

*Source*: Adapted from data in *Social Trends* 19 (1989), and reproduced with the permission of the Controller of Her Majesty's Stationery Office.

## A classification of group strategies

The sectional/cause distinction is of some value as a first step in group classification. However, there is also scope for a classification based on alternative group strategies, and on the receptivity of government to those strategies, which in turn has an impact on group effectiveness. One such classification is the insider group/outsider group division and its various subdivisions (Grant 1978, 1984). Insider groups are regarded as legitimate by government and are consulted on a regular basis. Outsider groups either do not wish to become enmeshed in a consultative relationship with officials, or are unable to gain recognition. Another way of looking at them is to see them as protest groups which have objectives that are outside the mainstream of political opinion. They then have to adopt campaigning methods designed to demonstrate that they have a solid basis of popular support, although some of the methods used by the more extreme groups may alienate potential supporters.

Although many insider groups will be sectional groups, cause groups can win insider status. For example, Ryan's (1978) study of the penal lobby shows that the Howard League for Penal Reform was treated as an insider group, in contrast to Radical Alternatives to Prison. Equally, there are sectional groups that have been outside the regular consultative system, such as the National Union of Ratepayers' Associations. For many years its main channel of access appeared to be the Post Office delivery boy who took their protest telegrams to the Treasury.

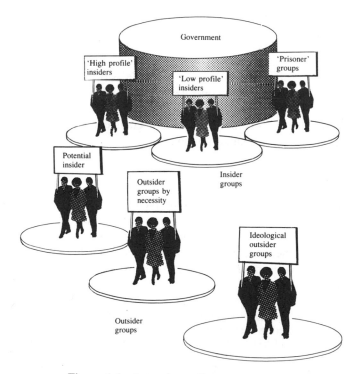

**Figure 1.1** A typology of pressure groups

The insider and outsider groups can each be subdivided into three categories. First there is the category of 'prisoner groups' who find it particularly difficult to break away from an insider relationship with government, either because they are dependent on government for assistance of various kinds (e.g. secondment of staff or office accommodation), or because they represent parts of the public sector (e.g. local authority associations or the chairmen of nationalised industries). Desperation at lack of success through normal channels may sometimes lead such groups to make a risky attempt to 'break out' but, unless they have exceptional resources, they are unlikely to survive 'on the outside' for very long.

The other two sub-types of insider group, 'low profile' and 'high profile', are based on the extent to which an organisation seeks to reinforce its contacts with government by using the mass media. In its most extreme form, the 'low profile' strategy would involve concentrating entirely on behind-the-scenes contacts with government and not making even routine statements to the mass media (e.g. the former British Employers' Confederation). A 'high profile' strategy involves a considerable emphasis on cultivating public opinion to reinforce contacts with government. The Confederation of British Industry (CBI) may be said to have shifted towards a 'high profile' strategy since 1974; the appearance of the organisation's director-general on the Jimmy Young Show may be seen as the high (or low) point of this new strategy. The staging of an annual conference of members is one sign of this attempt to appeal directly to public opinion.

## Outsider groups

Outsider groups as a category are by their nature more disparate than insider groups. The very fact of being an insider group imposes certain constraints and patterns of behaviour on a group. A group which does not abide by the rules may find itself excluded from the consultative process. Richardson (1977, p. 24) discusses a particular case of such exclusion:

> Contact with government departments . . . may be difficult to maintain; tact and discretion are at a premium in such matters. During the course of the National Parks campaign the SCNP [Standing Committee on National Parks] was invited to a meeting chaired by the Secretary of State for the Environment at which the SCNP representatives were too forceful in their criticisms. As a result they did not receive copies of the Consultation Paper which the department eventually prepared.

Like insider groups, outsider groups can be subdivided into three categories:

1. potential insider groups
2. outsider groups by necessity
3. ideological outsider groups.

Potential insider groups are those outsider groups which would like to become insider groups but have yet to win government acceptance. This can come in a number of ways. Pressure from Plaid Cymru MPs whose votes the Government needed to preserve its majority in the House of Commons led to the recognition of the Farmers' Union of Wales in the annual price review process in 1978. Friends of the Earth were invited to a meeting convened by the Secretary of State for the Environment after a campaign in which they dumped non-returnable bottles on the doorsteps of firms producing them.

More usually, however, insider status follows the adoption of a more responsible and conventional strategy of action by the group concerned. Elliott *et al.* (1982) show how the National Federation of the Self-Employed changed from an 'outsider' to an 'insider' organisation. In the late 1970s, the NFSE engaged in various forms of direct action, such as demonstrating outside the offices of Customs and Excise; there was very little direct contact with central government. From mid-1979 onwards, however, the picture changed, with a striking increase in committee work and direct contacts with government. By the autumn of 1980:

> there are no fewer than eleven committees busy holding meetings, calling for cases, talking to ministers and generally acting like 'insider' pressure groups who have established their legitimacy and now have relatively easy channels of communication with the centres of power. And at the same time there is reported only one example of 'direct action' in the 110 events identified as 'collective actions' ... The game has changed from protest to persuasion.
>
> (Elliott *et al.* 1982, p. 79)

Outsider groups by necessity may also wish to become insider groups, but they are less politically sophisticated than potential insider groups in terms of knowledge of how the political system works. Thus the distinction between these groups and potential interest groups is one of the level of political knowledge and skills available to the group. Clearly, the demarcation line between the two groups is not an insurmountable barrier, and outsider groups by necessity may become potential insider groups as their political skills improve.

Nevertheless, the distinction is an important one because it assists our understanding of the process whereby some outsider groups eventually become insider groups, thus uncovering some of the processes of change at work in the pressure group system. The basic point is that an interest group has to be able to deploy certain political skills before it can be accepted as an insider group. It has to show civil servants that it can (and is prepared to) talk 'their language'; that it knows how to present a case, and how to bargain and accept the outcome of the bargaining process. As the professional journal for pressure group executives has stated in an editorial, 'We have to learn the language and procedures of government and blend our work with it where necessary' (*Association Management, II*, 1980, p. 5).

The language of the British civil service is a language of veiled understatement and it is characteristic of politically sophisticated outsider groups that their demands are presented in strident terms. Their lack of understanding of the political system leads them to make demands which are constitutionally impossible. For example, the National Association of Ratepayer Action Groups, which spearheaded the 'ratepayers' revolt' of 1974, told the Layfield Committee that 'NARAG very seriously requests that, in any future Parliamentary debates on this subject, a free and open vote be taken; and that an amendment be added that no alteration of the agreed method be permitted at any time in the future without a similar free and open vote' (Layfield Report 1976, p 103).

Ideological outsider groups do not accept the possibility of achieving change through the existing political system. They adopt tactics which place them outside what is regarded as the normal spectrum of political activity. For example, the Animal Liberation Front has waged a violent campaign against butchers, fur shops, and scientists who use animals in experiments. Quite apart from the loss of activists through imprisonment, such organisations are prone to internal ideological arguments in which former allies become enemies (Porritt and Winner 1988, p. 53). Although their actions may win publicity, the debate may become one about their methods rather than their objectives.

May and Nugent have proposed an interesting modification to the insider/outsider distinction by suggesting that there is an intermediate category of 'thresholder' groups which exhibit 'strategic ambiguity and oscillation between insider and outsider strategies' (1982, p. 7). Some groups vary at times between a close relationship with government, and a more distant and adversarial one. May and Nugent suggest that trade unions may be analysed in these terms, pointing to the deterioration in the relationship between the unions and the government under the Heath Government of 1970 to 1974.

Unions do pose problems for pressure group analysis, in part because they are really secondary pressure groups: their principal function is collective bargaining with employers (the TUC is more of a conventional pressure group as compared with the individual unions, although it also has the function of trying to resolve inter-union disputes). Another factor is that many British unions are very decentralised organisations, so that sections of the membership may be pursuing a different strategy from the leadership. Ideological considerations may sometimes make it difficult for the TUC or individual trade unions to co-operate with the government on particular policies, such as training policy. However, they may not wish to relinquish the opportunity of influencing the detailed content and implementation of such policies. Indeed, strains about the appropriate strategy to adopt in the face of an unfriendly government are producing widening divisions within the trade union movement.

An implicit assumption of the insider/outsider distinction is that insider groups have a better chance of influencing government policy. Of course, particularly at an early stage of their development, some groups may have no alternative but to pursue an outsider strategy. A former campaign director of Friends of the Earth (FoE) has argued that traditional pressure group tactics are 'particularly useful for ... groups which have fairly high-level political or civil service contacts, and are able to activate an "old-boy network"' (Conroy 1981, p. 1). Groups pressing for radical changes in policy may find that they are regarded as cranks or that they lack 'clout' in terms of their technical credibility or political muscle. 'The "clout" exerted by FoE was directly proportional to the amount of public concern which it could generate' (p. 2). 'Controlled events' such as funeral processions for whales were a form of street theatre with an emotional theme calculated to induce anger, humour or sorrow. It is interesting that a civil servant commenting on these arguments suggested that demonstrations of the type favoured by FoE could give the organisation a frivolous appearance, while another civil servant argued that demonstrations could lead government to defer policy changes (Royal Institute of Public Administration 1981, p. 11).

## The gains offered by an insider strategy

In the longer run, most groups tend to veer towards an insider strategy because of the potential gains it offers. For example, Greenpeace has 'devoted more resources to research, to report-writing and to conventional lobbying techniques . . . These changes have in turn annoyed some of the direct action traditionalists, who fear loss of purity and effectiveness' (Edwards 1988, p. 17). Certainly, there are risks in exchanging independence for incorporation. Nettl argues that the 'British consensus' has the effect of emasculating pressure groups 'while preserving their outward shell of autonomy and independence' (Nettl 1965, p. 22). According to Elliott *et al.* (1982, p. 91) the National Federation of Self-Employed has accepted incorporation as the price to be paid for durability. Even more established groups may feel that they have paid too high a price for access to government. Isaac-Henry (1984, p. 145) comments in relation to local authority associations:

> Of course the associations must react to government initiatives, but they seem to be inexorably drawn into an all-embracing web of consultation which in essence makes them prisoners of the centre. There is a danger that when leading officials and members spend so much time with government officials and ministers they become servants of the centre, and their role is reduced to that of explaining government policy to member authorities.

In their study of the poverty lobby, Whiteley and Winyard (1987, p. 31) suggest that the insider/outsider distinction confuses the two separate dimensions of strategy and status. This leads them to suggest 'a distinction between open and focused to describe group strategies, and an accepted/non-accepted dimension to describe group status' (p. 31). By incorporating distinctions based on whether a group has a representational or service emphasis, and whether it is a group speaking *for* the poor or is made up *of* the poor, they build up four dimensional classifications for each group. The most common profiles are OPAL (open–promotional–acceptable–lobbying) and FRAS (focused–representational–acceptable–service) (p. 33).

This is a sophisticated and ingenious addition to the classification schemes to be found in the literature, but a defence can be mounted of the insider/outsider typology. First, some of the distinctions Whiteley and Winyard point to are catered for in the typology: for instance, differential use of the media is allowed for in the 'high profile' and 'low profile' sub-types within the insider group category. The notion of groups which 'pursue an "insider" strategy, but which are not acceptable to decision makers for Whitehall' is catered for in terms of the 'potential insider' groups. Above all, it is important to remember that, in practice, strategy and status are very closely interlinked, and it may be undesirable to separate them. Pursuing an insider strategy is a precondition of winning insider status, but often the apparent availability of insider status encourages the pursuit of an insider strategy. A new attentiveness to the claims of small business in the latter years of the 1974–9 Labour Government 'encouraged the routinisation of representation, discouraged small business leaders from taking any forms of direct action and enjoined them to model themselves on conventional lobbies' (Elliott *et al.* 1982, p. 84).

Above all, an important point about the insider/outsider strategy distinction is that it highlights the way in which the state sets the rules of the game for pressure group activity. Access and consultation flow from the adoption of a pattern of behaviour which is acceptable to government, particularly to civil servants. This creates incentives for groups to act in a particular way; pressure groups are thus tamed and domesticated with only the ideological rejectionists remaining outside the system.

## Pressure groups and democracy

There is a fundamental link between the existence of pressure groups and the very survival of a system of democratic government. Freedom of association is a fundamental principle of democracy. Democracy permits the existence of groups, but it could also be argued that groups contribute to the quality of the decision-making process. Those that have axes to grind may have something to say that is relevant to the issue under consideration.

A system of representative democracy offers electors a relatively infrequent choice between alternative party programmes. Systems which permit referenda to be held on specific issues extend the range of choice, but one consequence is often that the protagonists spend large sums of money on advertising to influence the outcome, with an unfair advantage being given to the side with more money. Pressure groups permit citizens to express their views on complex issues which affect their lives. In systems of voting, each vote counts equally, but numerical democracy can take no account of the *intensity* of opinion on a particular issue. Democracy cannot be simply reduced to a head-counting exercise: it must also take account of the strength of feelings expressed, and of the quality of arguments advanced. Moreover, group membership and activity offers an additional mechanism for citizens to participate in 'the experience of ruling and being ruled' (Lively 1975, p. 117).

This rather benign view of pressure group activity, which this author supports, can be challenged in two ways. It can be argued that pressure group activity simply reinforces existing patterns of political inequality in society. For example, consider the position of business in society. Business already has considerable influence over people's everyday lives because of the economic assets at its disposal, assets which allow it to make decisions about the location of plants, the range of products to be produced, the numbers and types of person to be employed, etc. Business is able to reinforce this economic power through pressure group activity, either at the level of the individual organisation (the firm), or through organisations representing particular industries or business as a whole.

Why is business allowed these dual advantages? At a fundamental level, it reflects a value choice by society, expressed through the outcome of elections, in favour of a capitalist, free-enterprise society. In that society, businesses are corporate citizens, paying taxes and being required to obey a wide variety of laws and regulations. It therefore does not seem unreasonable that business should be allowed an opportunity to express its views on public policies that affect it. On a practical level, it should be noted that there are two additional reasons why governments consult business interests. First, business can advise government on the practical consequences of a particular policy, thus helping government to avoid policies which are ineffective, or which have undesirable and unintended side effects. Second, business is often called on to assist in the implementation of a particular policy, such as a training policy, making it desirable to maintain its goodwill.

Even so, it can be argued that pressure groups which represent organisations rather than individuals have certain advantages in terms of their ability to exert effective influence on public policy. An institution has interests that are independent of its particular members, and its leadership has greater latitude in making decisions about how those interests can best be served. 'Institutions have less need to justify their political efforts by reference to membership approval or demand' (Salisbury 1984, p. 68). The significance of groups organising institutions is apparent when one considers that Rhodes *et al.* (1981) identified twenty-two associations representing local authorities, ranging from the Association of County Councils to the Federation of British Cremation Authorities.

More generally, it could be argued that groups which represent producers are usually more effectively organised than those which represent consumers. Contrast, for example, the organisation of business with the weakness of general consumer organisations; or the organisation of doctors with that of patients. This is not surprising when one considers that there is not really a consumer 'interest': rather, individual consumers have a wide range of interests flowing from their own particular needs and perspectives. For example, consider attitudes to public transport. Some consumers may prefer a market-oriented solution (privatisation of British Rail), others may prefer an increase in subsidies to public transport. Among the latter group, a regular user of Network South-East or the London Underground is going to have rather different priorities from those of a person who wants the bus service to his or her village restored, or who uses a publicly run shipping service to the Outer Hebrides.

Such problems make consumers difficult to organise. Work roles are more central to people's identity than their activity as consumers of a wide variety of products and services. Indeed, in some respects, this difference is a reflection of the extent to which groups are used to convey *intensity* of opinion. A farmer whose livelihood is threatened is likely to be more concerned about a new dairy regime than a consumer faced with paying an additional penny for a pint of milk.

One should not, however, dismiss too readily the concerns which have been expressed about the tendency for at least some pressure group activity to reinforce existing concentrations of power. However, it is difficult to take a position on these issues without having some general theory of the role of pressure groups in the policy-making process, and a number of alternative theories are set out in Chapter 2.

The other challenge that has been mounted to pressure groups questions their impact on the overall decision-making process in a society. In summary, it is argued by some liberal writers that the presence of what are referred to as *vested* interests makes it difficult to bring about necessary changes in a society. By mounting an effective defence of the status quo, group activity leads to ossification in a society. At the opposite end of the spectrum are the prescriptive corporatists who argue that a close relationship between groups and government is not only the most effective way of governing a polity, but also one that contributes to social progress. These alternative perspectives will also be considered more fully in Chapter 2.

# 2

# Pressure Groups and the Political System

This chapter reviews a number of alternative theoretical perspectives on the place of pressure groups in the political system. The focus is on theories which help us to understand the role of pressure groups in the democratic political process as a whole. Theories which consider, for example, the problems of recruiting or retaining group members, or the internal dynamics of interest groups, will be discussed only in so far as they are relevant to these broader issues.

One important point to bear in mind when reading about the various theories is the distinction between *analytical* and *normative* theories. There is, of course, a sense in which all theories are normative because the process of theory formation is not value free. Even so, a distinction can be maintained between those theories which set out to describe and explain a particular set of political phenomena, and those which seek to prescribe a preferred set of political arrangements: the distinction between 'is' and 'ought'.

One of the problems with pressure group theory is that this distinction between analytical and normative theories has often not been maintained, or at least has become confused in the minds of those writing about the subject. Consider corporatist theory, which is discussed more fully later in the chapter. Many of the writers on corporatism are prescriptive corporatists, that is, they believe that neo-corporatist arrangements enhance the quality of decision making in a democratic society, and that countries with such arrangements are, in general, better off than those without them. Other writers have been interested in corporatism simply as a means of trying to understand changes which took place in the relationship between the state and pressure groups in a number of western societies in the postwar period. They are not arguing that corporatist arrangements are particularly beneficial: simply that they have occurred, and need to be studied if we are to have a better understanding of the democratic process. However, the distinction between these two approaches often becomes blurred, so that analytical writers on the subject are often labelled 'corporatists' along with the prescriptive corporatists.

## Pluralism

Pluralism offers the most influential and resilient account of the role of pressure groups in a democratic society. In part, its resilience is due to its elasticity: pluralists hold a variety of positions, particularly on the role of the state in a democracy. According to Cox (1988a, p. 37), pluralism 'is a theory based in the notion that there is a lack of similarity of interests and styles shaping policies across the whole range of public policy-making'. Such a definition clearly covers a wide range of political situations which may be very different from each other. Even so, one of the key chracteristics of pluralism is the emphasis placed on the role of pressure groups in society as a means of providing access to the political system, and as a counterweight to undue concentrations of power. Thus, 'The pluralist case ... rests on the argument that the essential thing is competition and participation among organized *groups*, not among individuals' (Presthus 1964, p. 19).

Pluralist theory combines within it a mixture of normative and analytical elements: pluralist theorists often seem to be simultaneously offering both an account of how society ought to be organised, and a working model of how society is actually organised. In this description, pluralism will be treated as an analytical theory, but it should be emphasised that it has considerable normative undertones.

Pluralists believe that power in society is fragmented and dispersed. In particular, they believe that power is non-cumulative in the sense that those who are powerful in one area are not necessarily powerful in another. This idea of distinct issue areas has given rise to the neo-pluralist notion of 'policy communities' which is discussed more fully below. The dispersal of power is assisted by the presence of a large number of groups, and by the existence of a rough balancing equilibrium in the society which operates through the presence of 'countervailing' groups (e.g. labour countervails capital). If a particular interest is neglected, then a 'potential' group will be mobilised to represent it (see Truman 1951). This theory does have some practical relevance: in research on the CBI, Marsh and I discovered that its members thought that a principal reason for its existence was the need to provide a counterweight to the TUC, a consideration mentioned by almost every director we interviewed (Grant and March 1977, p. 49).

What must be stressed is that pluralists have never asserted that all groups have equal access to the political system and equal influence within it. Such a proposition would be absurd, as a political system organised on such lines would be in a constant state of paralysis, with each interest cancelled out by other interests. (See Jordan and Richardson 1987, p. 60 for a rebuttal of this criticism of pluralism.) Richardson and Jordan (1979, p. 13) use an analogy from economics to describe the mechanics of group competition:

> Just as in economics, 'perfect competition' rarely exists except in theory. In practice, we have at best an oligopolistic situation and at worst a monopolistic situation. In other words, groups attempt to manipulate the market in their favour. But they rarely succeed in achieving total control of the market (in our case total control of a particular policy area) for very long.

This analogy may be extended by examining the entry and exit barriers in the political market. Pluralist theory assumes that the entry barriers are relatively low, and that group mobilisation is relatively easy. Unfortunately, 'The flow in the pluralist heaven is that the heavenly chorus sings with a strong upper-class accent' (Schattschneider 1960, p. 35). It should also be remembered that exit barriers are relatively high in that the rate at which groups disappear is rather low. Moreover, groups formed in the past may have accumulated resources (of finance and reputation) which allow them to continue to exert an influence disproportionate to their contemporary importance. (This argument will be resumed when Olson's discussion of institutional sclerosis is reviewed later in the chapter.)

One other important point to bear in mind is that 'The major literature on pressure groups is . . . American. There is no major British contributor to theory' (Jordan and Richardson 1987, p. 53). One consequence is that pluralist theory often seems to reflect a more open, fragmented political system than applies in the case of Britain. In particular, government is often presented as highly fragmented. Such a picture has considerable validity in the US with its autonomous executive agencies, but less so in Britain. The notion of 'policy communities' has been developed largely by British theorists, and may offer a more accurate portrayal of the key features of the pressure group system in Britain.

## Pluralism: an assessment

Much of the pluralist case rests on the assumption that access to the political system is relatively easy, that forming a group which will be listened to is not particularly difficult. In 1965, Mancur Olson published a book called *The Logic of Collective Action* which appeared to cast doubt on some of the central assumptions made by pluralists. Olson argued that there was a logical flaw in the pluralists' treatment of economic interest groups. They assumed that individuals in a large group would make sacrifices to attain the political objectives of the group. Olson pointed out that the individual member of a large organisation was in a position where 'his own efforts will not have a noticeable effect on the situation of his organisation, and he can enjoy any improvements brought about by others whether or not he has worked in support of his organization' (Olson 1965, p. 16). Olson argued that the relatively small groups, which he termed 'privileged' or 'intermediate' groups, would be much easier to organise:

> The small oligopolistic industry seeking a tariff or tax loophole will sometimes attain its objective even if the vast majority of the population loses as a result. The smaller groups − the privileged and intermediate groups − can often defeat the large groups − the latent groups − which are normally supposed to prevail in a democracy.
>
> (Olson 1965, pp. 127−8)

Olson explained the existence of large numbers of groups in terms of a 'by-product theory' of pressure groups. Members did not join because of the collective goals the groups pursued, but because of the selective incentives (services. discounts, etc.) which were available only to members. Olson drew a picture of the pressure group system in which the business community was by far the best organised sector. It should be noted that Olson admitted that his theory did not apply to 'philanthropic' groups, where those organised were concerned about persons other than those organised in the group itself. It is in this area, of course, that there has been a considerable expansion of group activity since Olson wrote his book.

It would be no exaggeration to say that in the years after the publication of Olson's book, the study of pressure groups lived through 'The Olsonian years'. The debate about Olson's book is a complex one which it will only be possible to summarise here. One important distinction to emerge from the debate, however, is that between membership and participation. The cost of belonging to a group is generally relatively small as a proportion of a person's annual income or a firm's annual turnover; it is hardly worth being 'economically rational' about it. Moreover, as Moe points out, 'An individual may, for instance, derive a sense of satisfaction *from the very act of contributing*, when he sees this as an act of support for goals in which he believes' (1980, p. 188). Participation involves much higher costs in terms of the time expended (by an individual or an employee attending meetings in the firm's time), but it also brings greater benefits with it: the solidaristic benefits of participation, and privileged access to a shared exchange of information (the former is of greater importance in 'cause' groups, the latter in 'sectional' groups).

At a panel on interest groups at the 1988 annual meeting of the American Political Science Association, it was observed that there was now a need in the study of pressure groups to move 'beyond Olson-type questions'. Olson's book did, however, stimulate a much needed debate on why people join pressure groups, which is relevant to pluralist assumptions about the ease of group formation. What is apparent, if one looks at a reference book like the Directory of British Associations, is that there is a large and diverse number of organisations in modern Britain. Many of these are, of course, not pressure groups at all, and some are secondary rather than primary pressure groups (in the terms of the language used in Chapter 1). However, there are relatively few sectional interests or causes which are not catered for at all. On the sectional side, there are associations for drum manufacturers, for Catholic teachers, for the makers of miners' lamps, for Scottish pre-cast concrete manufacturers, and for registrars of births, marriages and deaths. The causes to which one can subscribe include: a body seeking to obtain the acceptance of chiropractic techniques within the National Health Service; an organisation seeking to secure a reassessment of the role of King Richard III in British history; a society seeking to preserve the character and beauty of the Sussex Downs; or the Zionist Federation of Great Britain and Ireland.

It must be emphasised again that pluralists would not claim that all these groups have equal access and influence in the political system. Much would depend on changing values within society, which might enhance the importance of some issues and diminish others. For example, the issue of smoking is much more at the centre of the political stage in the 1980s than previously. Hence, a group like ASH (Action on Smoking and Health) is no longer seen as a marginal and rather cranky organisation. Indeed, a group supported by the tobacco industry has been set up to promote the rights of smokers, drawing on values of freedom of choice to counteract those related to a healthy life style and preventive medicine. The trade unions are less influential in the 1980s than they were in the 1970s, partly because of a change of government, but also because of a growing public perception that unions were abusing the influence given to them under the 'postwar settlement' which legitimised their role in the political process.

Shifts in influence in response to changes in public opinion are consistent with notions of democracy (although there are difficult issues about how people's views are formed in the first place which would require a book by themselves). Evidence of the existence of systematic biases raises more serious problems. Offe and Wiesenthal (1985) have argued that there are 'two logics of collective action'. Labour is powerless unless it organises: organised action is only one of a number of alternatives open to employers. It is also evident that there are some key groups in society which are relatively poorly organised, including the unemployed, the homeless, retired persons, and young people on state training schemes.

Another set of problems arises from the absence of democracy within pressure groups themselves. Either arrangements for democratic control are limited, or they tend to fall into disuse. Control of an organisation can pass into a self-perpetuating oligarchy. Activists tend to be those who have the time and money to devote to organisational work, so that doctors' organisations may have a disproportionate number of doctors with private practices in leadership positions, whilst farmers' organisations may be led by the better-off arable farmers who can afford to be away from their farms. However, such leaderships must be careful not to move too far away from the opinions of their members, or they may lose large segments of the membership, as, for example, in the case of the separate organisation of a Welsh Farmers' Union.

A more fundamental criticism of pluralism is that there are two levels of power in society, and that pluralism really only tells us about the lower level. The upper level is that of the core assumptions of society, such as private property, which largely go unquestioned. These core assumptions set the terms of reference for conflicts and outcomes at the lower level where 'the picture will look something like the polygon of forces found by pluralist analysis' (Westergaard and Resler 1976, p. 248). It could be argued, however, that if the core assumptions of society are to be challenged, it should be done through the party system where electors can be offered a radical alternative to the status quo (such as that offered by the Green Party). Within government itself, the battle for resources between different departments does, in some senses, resemble a competition between particular institutionalised interests (health, education, industry, agriculture, etc.).

## Policy communities

The notion of a policy community represents a useful adaptation of the pluralist notion of distinct issue areas to the particular circumstances of modern British government. The basic idea is that 'The policy-making map is in reality a series of vertical compartments of segments — each segment inhabited by a different set of organised groups, and generally impenetrable by "unrecognised groups" or the general public' (Richardson and Jordan 1979, p. 174). Policy communities are generally organised around a government department and its network of client groups. The real divisions are between the different policy communities, rather than within the communities themselves, where there is 'an interpenetration of department and client groups' (p. 44).

The relevance of the idea of policy communities can be illustrated by reflecting for a moment on health and agricultural policy making. The president of the National Farmers' Union (NFU) and the general secretary of the British Medical Association (BMA) are key actors in the agricultural and medical policy communities respectively. They will have intensive contacts with ministers and senior civil servants in the Ministry of Agriculture, Fisheries and Food on the one hand, and the Department of Health on the other. However, if the general secretary of the BMA attempted to intervene in the fixing of intervention prices for dairy products, he might be deemed to require help from members of his profession practising psychiatric medicine. Even if he were trying to argue that high levels of butter consumption are bad for public health, he might be seen as making an unwarrantable intrusion into matters not of his concern. Equally, if the president of the NFU expressed an opinion on the working hours of junior doctors, some of his own members might suggest an early rest cure. Policy making is highly compartmentalised and this tendency has been increasing with the growing intrusion of highly technical matters on the policy-making agenda, particularly stimulated by the expanding importance of the European Community.

It must be emphasised that the notion of a community does not imply that there is an absence of conflict, any more than there would be complete and undisturbed harmony in a geographical community. In their classic study of the 'Whitehall village', Heclo and Wildavsky note (1974, p. xv) that 'Community refers to the personal relationships between major political and administrative actors – sometimes in conflict, often in agreement, but always in touch and operating within a shared framework.' It must also be emphasised that policy communities differ from one another in their characteristics. Cox, Lowe and Winter (1986a, p. 16) characterise 'The policy community for rural conservation . . . as large, diverse and pluralistic; that for agriculture as small, tightly-knit and corporatist.' This particular contrast will be discussed again in Chapter 7, where a case study of agriculture and the environment is presented.

As an analytical proposition, the idea of policy communities clearly provides a good fit with the available empirical evidence on how decisions are made in British government. The existence of such policy communities does, however, raise some worrying problems for normative democratic theory. It is clear that these policy communities have rather high entry barriers around them (although the entry barriers are probably higher in longer-established communities such as agriculture than in younger ones such as conservation). Policy communities can become rather exclusive networks made up of well-established 'insider' groups. Richardson and Jordan comment (1979, p. 174): 'One cost involved in the increasingly close relationship between groups and government is that the policy process has if anything excluded the general public from any effective influence.' What emerges is rather like an élite cartel in which participants collude to preserve the existing parameters of the policy-making process. Not only is the range of participants limited, but there are good grounds for concern about the quality of the decision-making process. Stringer and Richardson (1982, p. 22) argue that 'The objective of the policy-making process within these communities is often not the solving of real problems, but the management of avoidance of conflict, the creation or maintenance of stable relationships, and the avoidance of abrupt policy changes.'

## Corporatism

Corporatist theories of pressure group activity have provoked considerable controversy in recent years. (The term neo- or liberal corporatism is often used to distinguish corporatism from its earlier association with fascism.) Indeed, Jordan and Richardson (1987, p. 95) go so far as to argue that 'the mainspring of the corporatist attack, Philippe Schmitter, created a divisive debate where none need have existed'. Cox (1988a) argues that Schmitter has attracted a group of disciples who have failed to follow developments in Schmitter's thinking.

One of the main limitations of the corporatist debate has been a lack of agreement, among those taking part in it, about what the term means. For example, some writers would like to restrict it to tripartite arrangements involving government, business and labour, whilst others would wish to include bilateral arrangements between, for exmaple, government and a profession. What is clear is that corporatist arrangements are confined to organisations arising from the division of labour in society, that is, producer groups, including professional organisations. It should also be noted that corporatist arrangements are linked with a relatively interventionist role by the state in society, even if it is regarded as nothing more than a 'social partner' alongside organised business and organised labour.

In practice, many corporatist arrangements have arisen from the politics of a prices and incomes policy which has led government into new bargaining relationships with organised business and organised labour. A corporatist relationship, however, involves something more than close and intense consultation with particular interest groups, offering business and labour a share in the making of economic policy. It also leads to the pressure groups being involved in the implementation of policy. In particular, they are required to secure the compliance of their members in the implementation of negotiated agreements (e.g. price restraint, income restraint, new training policies). The pressure groups thus become intermediaries of a new kind between their members and the state, not simply articulating their members' views to government, but sharing in the development of policy, and acquiring a responsibility for its implementation which may include the disciplining of members. Thus, for example, in 1976 the TUC was able to forestall a threatened seamen's strike which would have undermined the government's incomes policy by hinting that the National Union of Seamen might be expelled from the TUC.

It is thus important to distinguish between, on the one hand, negotiations where a pressure group and the government argue over the content of a proposed policy (a new tax proposal or a new environmental regulation) and where the outcome is influenced by such factors as the government's determination to pursue a particular policy, the strength of the group's case, and the political resources at its disposal; and on the other hand, negotiations where, in return for being given a share in policy making, the group is required to 'deliver' the consent of its members. There is a difference between involving pressure groups in discussions leading up to the annual budget, and making the implementation of part of that budget conditional on a particular response from a group. Thus, in the 1976 Budget, 'income tax cuts from 35 per cent to 33 per cent in basic rate were made conditional on the success of the pay talks with the TUC on Stage II of wage restraint' (Holmes 1985, p. 84).

In general, three main criticisms have been made of corporatist theories:

1. They are insufficiently distinguished from, or add little to, the pluralist theories they seek to supplant or supplement; at best, they might be described as a subtype of pluralism.
2. Empirical examples of corporatism, either at the national or sectoral level, are much more difficult to find than has been claimed.
3. Corporatist arrangements are responsible for many of the problems encountered by the British economy in the twentieth century.

The argument that corporatist theories are insufficiently distinguished from pluralist theories gains some force from the fact that writers on corporatism admit that the two bodies of theory share some common assumptions (Schmitter 1979). What is clear is that 'The role of the state is ... central to the concept of corporatism' (Cawson 1986, p. 36). Collective bargaining between employers and labour, for example, is not corporatism unless there is a significant state presence. It is argued that 'pluralism never had a theory of the state; it took the theory of representative government as adequate for that' (p. 26).

Corporatist writers have, until recently, not had a great deal to say on the question of the state. For example, there has been little exploration of state structure, or of the possibility that the function of interest intermediation might be discharged by the state itself, as in the sponsorship divisions within the Department of Trade and Industry (now abolished). Moreover, when corporatists do write about the state they come up against the problem that one of their assumptions has been a blurring of the public—private distinction with the proliferation of bodies and organisations that are not unambiguously part of either the state or civil society. Indeed, Schmitter (1985, pp. 32—3) argues that 'Most of the conditions that previously allowed theorists to treat the state as a distinctive social institution are no longer present to the same degree.' Indeed, all that is left 'is an amorphous complex of agencies with ill-defined boundaries, performing a great variety of not very distinctive functions' (p. 33).

### What does corporatism tell us about British politics?

In assessing the extent to which corporatist phenomena can actually be encountered in the British political process, it is important to remember that corporatism is an ideal type: only approximations of corporatist-type arrangements can be expected to be found in the real world. It is clear that tripartite arrangements were more central to the policy-making process in Britain in the 1970s than in the 1980s. (This applied to the Heath Government after 1972 as much as to the Labour Government in 1974—9.) But one point that should be made immediately is that tripartite arrangement fell far short of the corporatist ideal in so far as the CBI and the TUC often had great difficulty in implementing agreements. As Marsh and Grant (1977, p. 206) commented:

> It is evident . . . that both the CBI and the TUC have weaknesses which make it doubtful whether they could function effectively as pillars of a tripartite system . . . it is by no means certain that either group, once it has entered into an agreement, can ensure that its members accept that agreement as authoritative. Neither group is more than a coalition of more or less diverging interests.

These observations were later echoed by participants in the political process at the time. As Joel Barnett, Chief Secretary to the Treasury in the 1974—9 Labour Cabinet notes, 'We frequently paid a high price to obtain the cooperation of our trade union friends' (Barnett 1982, p. 33). The Conservatives were able to claim that the Government traded permanent legislative concessions for temporary agreements on incomes policy.

The Conservative Government since 1979 has broken away from this style of policy making. Institutions such as the National Economic Development Council (NEDC) have been downgraded, whilst intermediaries which played a key role in the 1970s such as the 'Neddy

Six' (the TUC members of the NEDC who negotiated with government on behalf of the trade unions) have disappeared altogether. The sponsorship divisions which handled relations with particular sectors of industry within the Department of Trade and Industry have been abolished. Lord Young, the former Trade and Industry Secretary, has claimed: 'We have rejected the TUC; we have rejected the CBI. We do not see them coming back again. We gave up the corporate state' (*Financial Times*, 9 November 1988).

The Government takes the position that corporatism is one of the causes of Britain's poor economic record in the past. In a 1988 White Paper it was claimed that:

> The ability of the economy to change and adapt was hampered by the combination of corporatism and powerful unions. Corporatism limited competition and the birth of new firms whilst, at the same time, encouraging protectionism and restrictions designed to help existing firms.
>
> (Cm. 278, p. 1)

This revelation of the extent of corporatism's impact on the economy came as a surprise to academic analysts who thought that Britain represented an example of failed attempts at corporatism rather than of the malign and widespread effects of corporatism in action. Ever since the 'productioneer' movement at the end of the First World War (Davenport-Hines 1984) there have been advocates of corporatist solutions to Britain's problems. The nearest Britain came to such an arrangement was under the Heath Government from 1972 to 1974. However, despite the enthusiasm of the Prime Minister, even this attempt failed. Tripartism is unlikely to be revived in the future, although fears have been expressed from the right of the political spectrum that the political integration of Europe could let corporatism in through the back door (Catholic social theory is one of the mainsprings of corporatist thought, and continental Christian Democratic parties tend to take a more benign view of co-operating with the 'social partners' than the British Conservatives).

As someone who has been labelled a 'disciple' (Cox 1988a, p. 39) of Philippe Schmitter (the correct Californian terminology is 'supporting actor'), should I take this opportunity to apologise for the shortcoming of corporatist analysis? As I have never been a prescriptive corporatist in relation to Britain, my feelings of guilt are somewhat limited. It is, admittedly, unfortunate that 'corporatism' is used rather loosely in the press as a term of abuse for past political failings; the academic participants in the debate must share some of the blame (although not too much) for failing to define the term more precisely.

If there is a criticism which can be made of the corporatist debate, it is that academic analysts responded too slowly to changes that were taking place in the relationship between the state and interest organisations in a number of West European societies. By the time they had developed a conceptual apparatus to analyse the phenomenon, and had managed to organise large-scale research projects, the object of study was already dwindling in importance. The corporatist debate did, however, help to stimulate a new wave of theoretical and empirical work on pressure groups, prompting a re-examination of pluralist theory, and thereby encouraging the development of new forms of pluralist analysis such as the idea of policy communities.

## The liberal critique of pressure groups

The study of pressure groups in Britain was pioneered by two American political scientists, Samuel Beer (1956, 1965) and Harry Eckstein (1960). Their starting point was the American pluralist perspective on pressure gorups, but they also found in Britain an older corporatist tradition which reinforced the legitimacy of group activity. Their view, then, of the pressure group system in Britain was essentially a benign one, although Beer took a more pessimistic view in a later (1982) work. Their view was echoed by a leading British writer on pressure groups of the period, Finer (1958), who concluded his book with a plea for 'Light, more light!', that is, more information and openness about the operation of the pressure group system.

This benign view happened to be reinforced by wider developments in political life. The year 1960 saw the so-called Brighton Revolution. This marked a shift towards a more interventionist approach to the management of the economy which went beyond the aggregate demand management of the 1950s. (For an excellent analysis of this shift, see Hall 1986, Chapter 4.) The Brighton Revolution specifically refers to a conference of what amounted to the economic establishment of the country held at Brighton in November 1960 by the Federation of British Industries, against the background of increasing concern about Britain's economic performance. It led to a new enthusiasm for a limited form of economic planning among business leaders. (An excellent short account of the Brighton Revolution and its consequences is to be found in Brittan 1964, pp. 238–45.)

The significance of what developed into a shift to incomes policies and industrial policies was that it necessarily involved government in a closer relationship with key producer groups. The role of incomes policy in encouraging a tripartite style of government—industry relations has already been discussed earlier in the chapter. Sectoral industrial policies usually draw government closer to pressure groups because their success 'is dependent on how readily producer groups will agree to accept the inevitable dislocations associated with economic adjustment' (Atkinson and Coleman 1985, p. 27).

The 1970s saw the collapse of the post-war Keynesian consensus, and its eventual replacement by a new monetarist orthodoxy. The exact reasons for this collapse do not concern us here, nor does the timing of the collapse or the extent to which the 1974—9 Labour Government repudiated Keynesianism. The first oil shock of 1973, alongside serious industrial disputes in Britain, precipitated the crisis of Keynesianism, but it can be argued that these particular events simply revealed more fundamental flaws in Keynesian political economy.

In any event, a new critique of pressure group activity emerged. It should be noted that this critique emerged against a background of considerable economic and political disruption, constituting the most serious crisis in Britain's post-war history. The rate of inflation in 1975 was 24.2 per cent. Two senior retired military officers formed 'private armies' which could be called upon in the event of a collapse of law and order in Britain. There was even speculation about the possibility of a military coup. Indeed, it is now known that elements in MI5 were plotting against the Prime Minister, Harold Wilson, who for some reason was perceived as a radical threat to the status quo.

This background has been sketched in to suggest that the time was ripe for some new thinking about the durability and viability of the post-war political settlement in Britain, which involved a new emphasis being given to the role of pressure groups, particularly trade unions, in the political process. Indeed, a general debate about British 'ungovernability' was sparked off, although this has not stood the test of time very well given that Mrs Thatcher has shown that the British state has considerable powers at its disposal if it is directed by someone with strong and clear political convictions.

The most important piece of writing to appear at the time on the subject of pressure groups was an article by Samuel Brittan (1975). Brittan argued that liberal representative democracy was threatened by the generation of excessive expectations, and the disruptive effects of the pursuit of group self-interest. Producer groups had not in the past made full use of their potential power, 'but have tended to make increasing use of it as time has passed'. Brittan was particularly concerned about the activities of trade unions, which differed from other organised groups in terms of their willingness to withdraw output from the market until paid more. The kinds of demand being made strained to breaking point the 'sharing out' function of democratic society.

The particular problem of what was perceived to be excessive trade union power has apparently been resolved by a number of actions taken by the Thatcher Government: a series of reforms in employment law; a willingness to hold out against strikes by key public sector groups; encouragement of more decentralised forms of bargaining, a trend which privatisation may facilitate; and the consequences of rising unemployment in the 1980s at a time when unions still felt that they had considerable potential power. One should also note the structural shift in the economy, which has led to a declining employment share of traditionally unionised sectors such as manufacturing.

### Samuel Brittan's critique of pressure groups

Samuel Brittan has provided through his later work a more general critique of the role of pressure groups in democracy from the perspective of an economic liberal. His arguments are a healthy corrective to a period when extensive pressure group activity was seen as an inevitable part of a modern democracy. Although he occasionally does have some good things to say about pressure groups, Brittan may be regarded as an extreme critic of such organisations. His perspective is, however, based on a wish to defend the values of freedom and an open society. Reviewing an influential critique of pressure group activity which he wrote in the mid-1970s (Brittan 1975), Brittan reflected (1987a, p. 14):

> My theme ... became the incompatible claims of rival interest groups which increase in influence when government takes on overambitious economic functions. Interest groups do not merely reduce the national income when they become embedded in the political process. They embody rival claims which more than exhaust the national product and threaten the survival of liberal democracy itself.

Brittan argues (1987b, p. 79) that interest group pressure constitutes one of a number of threats to individual freedom and popular government. Analysing the interest group threat, he notes (p. 74) that 'The main theme of Hayek's latest work is that democracy has degenerated into an unprincipled auction to satisfy rival organised groups who can never in the long run be appeased because their demands are mutually incompatible.' Brittan's clear message (pp. 262—3) is that 'the entrenched position of industrial, economic and political interest groups will limit what can be achieved by any form of economic management, new or old'. Constitutional and political reform is necessary to reduce the role of interest groups and increase that of the individual citizen.

It might appear that with Mrs Thatcher's declared opposition to 'vested interests', and her distaste for any kind of corporatism, such a programme of reform is under way. Certainly, the power of the trade unions has been reduced, and Brittan would argue that the problems identified in his 1975 article now apply to the pressures on the US government to 'do something' about the trade deficit (Brittan 1987a, p 19). However, Brittan is clearly of the view that Mrs Thatcher's Government has done very little to reduce certain areas of middle-class privilege. He notes, 'Many interest group privileges, for instance for pension funds, mortgage holders or concessions to farmers, appear as tax reliefs' (Brittan 1989, p. 17). Indeed, one could extend Brittan's argument by arguing that Mrs Thatcher has been willing to take on 'soft' targets like opticians and the system of house conveyancing, but has avoided politically more difficult targets like mortgage interest relief. Even in the privatisation programme, the Government has been very willing to make concessions to the existing managements of nationalised industries so that it has often ended up with private monopolies.

## Olson's argument and the historical evidence

Another important contribution to the liberal critique of interest groups has been made by Mancur Olson (1982). Indeed, Brittan notes that 'There was a natural link between my thesis on collective pressures on democracy and the Mancur Olson thesis that the longer a country has enjoyed stable democratic political institutions, the more time there will be for interest group coalitions to form, which undermine performance' (Brittan 1987a, p. 15). Olson argues that stable societies with unchanged boundaries tend to accumulate more special interest organisations over time. The general effect is to reduce efficiency and aggregate income, and a society's capacity to reallocate resources and adopt new technology in response to changing conditions. Olson admits that a broadly based, 'encompassing' organisation has an important incentive to take account of the consequences of its actions on the society as a whole. He points out, however, that many of the 'peak associations' studied by political scientists lack sufficient unity to produce coherent policy.

Britain has a particularly powerful network of special interest organisations, a phenomenon which Olson links to Britain's poor growth record. 'British society has acquired so many strong organizations and collusions that it suffers from an institutional sclerosis that slows its adaptation to changing circumstances and technologies' (Olson 1982, p. 78). He concludes that special interests are 'harmful to economic growth, full employment, coherent government, equal opportunity and social mobility' (p. 237). One possible remedy might be the repeal of 'all special-interest legislation or regulation and at the same time [the application of] rigorous anti-trust laws to every type of cartel or collusion that uses its power to obtain prices or wages above competitive levels' (p. 236).

Much of what we know about the history of pressure group activity would seem to support Olson's argument. It has already been argued that the number of pressure groups has tended to grow over time, and that the exit barriers preserving groups tend to be higher than the entry barriers in the way of new group formations. It would also seem to fit in with much of what we know of inter-war economic history, particularly when viewed from the perspective of the 'institutional' school of economic historians (Elbaum and Lazonick 1986). This was an important period in Britain's economic development because a recognition of the problem of poor British economic performance was accompanied by only partially successful attempts to do anything about it. Lazonick's (1986) study of the cotton industry, for example, shows what can only be described as an appalling degree of institutional rigidity, with structures shaped by Victorian moulds.

However, it is possible to construct an account of the inter-war period (drawing again on the insights of the 'institutional' school) which would start with the failure of the 'productioneers', with their advocacy of new forms of government—industry relationship, to win the political battle over the form of post-war reconstruction. Hence, organisations sponsored by the government, such as the British Iron and Steel Federation, degenerated into cartels beyond state control because government was unwilling or unable to intervene more effectively to influence their activities.

Olson's analysis also does not account for the Restrictive Trade Practices Act of 1956, which transformed the functions of many associations by prohibiting them from acting as price-fixing and market-sharing cartels (indeed, some organisations disappeared altogether).

Following the passage of this Act, 'many associations had to adapt themselves, if they were to justify their existence, to more positive activities' (Devlin Commission 1972, p. 24).

Nevertheless, Olson's analysis is of value in pointing to a problem of political adjustment in countries like Britain. Older industries were able to develop a dense network of institutional protections (a well-developed, closed 'policy community' to use one language of analysis) which enabled them to slow down the transfer of resources to newer industries through protectionist measures, government subsidies, etc.

Where his analysis is more open to question is in relation to the argument that Britain was particularly afflicted by such problems. Just as some analysts tend to exaggerate the extent to which German industry was devastated by the Second World War, so Olson tends to overstate the institutional 'clean break' that occurred in Germany and Japan (see Olson 1982, p. 76). Lynn and McKeown (1988, p. 173) argue that 'Olson very much exaggerates the extent to which special interest groups were abolished in Japan under the rule of the militarists during the war and under the Occupation after it.' Similar continuities may be observed in Germany (Grant, Paterson and Whitston 1988; Streeck 1983, p. 143). A broader, cross-national study also suggests considerable elements of continuity in countries disrupted during the war by defeat or occupation (Grant, Nekkers and van Waarden, forthcoming).

The liberal critique of pressure group activity has obliged those of us who take a relatively benign view of organised interests to re-examine some of our fundamental assumptions. The liberal analysis has helped to revitalise the analysis of pressure groups in so far as it was becoming increasingly focused on relatively narrow questions such as the merits of different typologies of pressure groups. Even if one does not agree with their particular analysis, writers like Brittan and Olson have made an important contribution towards lifting the debate on to a higher plane. They have redirected our attention towards broader issues such as the relationship between pressure group activity and basic societal goals like the preservation of freedom and economic success. As Brittan (1987a, p. 15) notes:

> The dilemma is that many of the same groups − e.g. trade associations, unions, farmers, clubs or users' councils − which appear in political theory as beneficient intermediate associations betwen the citizen and the state, and the very cement of democracy, appear in political economy as threats to economic performance and stability.

## The Tory defence of interest

The liberal critique of interest group activity, imperfectly reflected in Thatcherite thinking and action, stands in strong contrast to the traditional Tory analysis of the role of interest organisations in society. This traditional Tory or moderate Conservative strand was once the dominant tendency in the Conservative Party, but has been supplanted since 1979 by Thatcherite neo-liberalism. However, a number of influential Conservatives, including some possible successors to Mrs Thatcher, have a background in 'one nation' conservatism. It may become more influential again in the future, although post-Thatcherite conservatism will probably be a blend of Thatcherism and more traditional conservatism — what is sometimes called 'third force' conservatism.

Tories reject the atomistic individualism inherent in neo-liberalism, and see interests as necessary and desirable intermediaries between the individual and society as a whole. Whilst not necessarily accepting the Thatcherite view that there is no such thing as society, that is, that society is a totally artifical construct, they would argue that the individual cannot experience society as a whole. Organisations which link the individual to a wider community are valuable both for engendering a corporate spirit and for the communal good that they achieve. Indeed, the traditional Tory view comes close to being a prescriptive corporatist one, with its emphasis on the role of interests in governance, and proposals for an 'industrial Parliament'. (This is a recurrent Conservative theme: see Churchill, 1930; Amery, 1947; Gilmour, 1983.)

The most articulate exponent of the Tory interpretation of interests in the 1970s and 1980s has been Sir Ian Gilmour. He argues that 'Tories were ... never enthusiasts for *laissez-faire* with its glorification of individual self-interest and its distrust of groups' (Gilmour 1983, p. 203). 'A Tory, then, rejects the simple idea that individuals are selfish and good and groups selfish and bad' (p. 204). That is not to say that Gilmour views all groups benignly. He has been very critical of the British trade union movement, arguing for the need 'to make trade-union activity less self-destructive and to bring home to the average trade-unionist that union power is only legitimate within limits' (Gilmour 1978, p. 239). However, he is also very critical of the CBI, which he portrays as weak, divided, lacking in political intelligence and sophistication, and subservient to the Conservative Party (Gilmour 1983, pp. 194–5, 207). More generally, Gilmour echoes earlier arguments about the role of interest groups by arguing that their activities should be made more visible, with greater democratic influence being exerted over them (p. 208).

Conservatives have, then, emphasised what Ian Macleod, in a speech to the 1958 Conservative Party conference, called the relationship between the 'great partners — the Government, the trade unions and the employers' (quoted in Gilmour 1983, p. 195). It is the Conservatives who have set up tripartite institutions such as the National Economic Development Council (NEDC) and the Manpower Services Commission (MSC). The contrast between Mrs Thatcher's neo-liberalism and the traditional Tory approach is illustrated by the fact that she downgraded the NEDC and abolished the MSC.

## Socialist views of pressure groups

There is not really a socialist view of pressure group activity, although advocates of state planning argue that 'The superiority of the collectivist economy, and particularly that of Soviet Russia, lies in the fact that, by planning, it has been possible to integrate the pressure groups into the pursuit of a social ideal' (Oulès 1966, p. 105). In the state socialist societies of Eastern Europe, there have not, until very recently, been pressure groups in the western sense, although that does not mean that there are no distinctive and well-organised interests (note, for example, the Roman Catholic Church in Poland). (For a comparative analysis of pressure groups in eastern and western countries, see Ball and Millward 1986.) Organised interests are starting to emerge in East European countries as their societies change. For example, I was invited to an East European country to address an organisation which had recently been given the task of interest intermediation by its government.

Centre-left post-war Labour governments in Britain, because of their wish to manage the economy, have tended to veer towards a weak form of prescriptive corporatism. This has been marked by intensive consultations with the unions and the employers (although, as noted above, all the significant tripartite institutions were set up by Conservative governments). There have also been some half-hearted attempts by Labour governments to improve the position of underorganised interests, for example with the formation of the National Consumer Council. In general, however, the impression that emerges from reading the many books by former Labour ministers is the extent to which they took an orthodox approach to pressure groups. That is to say, they viewed them as a legitimate part of the political system which had to be consulted, although this might often become a chore. They were certainly irritated by organisations which went outside the conventional channels and resorted to demonstrations. In general, however, they worked the system as they had inherited it, although developing it through closer partnership relationships with selected pressure groups.

A distinctive approach to pressure groups was taken by some Labour-controlled metropolitan local authorities (particularly in London). There was sometimes a conscious startegy of ignoring traditional middle-class pressure groups (conservation societies, etc.). On the other hand, priority was given to funding, organising and responding to what were perceived as deprived groups in society such as ethnic minorities and sexual minorities. Local authority activities in the latter area proved to be particularly controversial, and probably did the party some electoral damage.

## Technostructure

Pross has adapted Galbraith's notion of the technostructure to the study of pressure groups, the technostructure being defined as 'a sophisticated communications network of technically proficient specialists that cuts across the lines dividing government and business and in which technical knowledge is the currency of power' (Pross 1986, p. 49). Pross's study is particularly important because it links together a number of the ideas discussed in this chapter and elsewhere in this book.

Pross places particular emphasis on the notion of the 'policy community'. He sees the core, the policy-making centre, of each policy community as being made up 'primarily of government agencies and institutionalized interest groups' (p. 98). Thus, one has sub-governments which constitute the policy makers in a particular area made up of very small groups of people. The other segment of the policy community is the 'attentive public'. The attentive public is less tightly knit or well defined. It includes government agencies, pressure groups, academics, consultants and journalists, 'who are affected by, or interested in, the policies of specific agencies and who follow, and attempt to influence, those policies, but do not participate in policy-making on a regular basis' (p. 99). The attentive public should not be disregarded, however, because it contributes to the shaping of the policy agenda, perpetually reviewing the development of policy.

Pross's contribution goes beyond drawing attention to the existence of two segments in the policy community. He traces a link between the growth of a bureaucratised state and the bureaucratisation of pressure groups. Pross argues that 'the natural constituency for bureaucracy is the sectorally oriented policy community' (p. 209). Pressure groups developed their own bureaucracies to mirror those of government, and the growth of the pressure group bureaucracies identified new areas in which pressure group activity took place. Government, for its part, found the groups useful partners for both formulation and implementation of policy (pp. 39–45).

Interdependence led to the sophisticated communications network characteristic of the technostructure. The increasing dominance of technical competence in the policy process had, according to Pross (p. 49), important implications for democracy:

> First ... it 'short-circuited' traditional institutions of political representation. Second, it changed the language of policy-making in a fashion that excluded lay people, including politicians. Third, in promoting neutral competence, it denigrated political participation in both administration and policy-making and substituted for it technical expertise.

Pross maintains that 'specialized bureaucracies and their surrounding policy communities are powerful — conceivably powerful enough to be, *de facto*, the paramount system of representation' (p. 209). A situation in which 'policy specialization accords to a relatively small public a dominant say in the creation and implementation of policy' (p. 272) raises important questions about democracy. Pross does go on to argue that the policy community is not impervious to change, and that the attentive public is able to challenge existing policy. This fits in with Whiteley and Winyard's argument (1987, p. 10) that 'group influence can be exerted by use of the media and by trying to change the intellectual climate surrounding a particular issue'. The use of the media by groups is discussed in Chapter 4 but it should be noted that Pross cautions that the dynamic for change arising within the attentive public is not spontaneous and requires deliberate encouragement.

It should also be noted that policy communities vary in their characteristics. For example, some are more tightly knit and impervious to outside influences than others. (Differences between policy communities will be analysed in Chapter 7.) It should also be remembered that some important issues in effect become clashes between policy communities, represented by their government departments: for example, between agriculture and environment, or between agriculture and health.

The particular importance of Pross's work is that he reminds us that the world of insider groups and relatively closed policy communities is not something that is the result of a historical accident which could be easily reversed, but rather is the consequence of the interrelationship of a number of linked processes. Bureaucratisation encourages the proliferation of expertise; the policy debate becomes a relatively closed and technical one; and much policy making is in effect delegated to particular arenas away from the centre of government and public scrutiny. As one reviewer of Pross has commented, 'A democratic system of governance should provide some means whereby groups and classes who do not normally gain access to sub-governments can question their usually private decisions' (Coleman 1987, p. 622). These issues will be considered again in the concluding chapter.

# 3

# How Pressure Groups Influence Whitehall and the Political Agenda

Pressure groups do not have the power to make authoritative decisions themselves. They do not constitute governments, or control legislatures, or staff courts. Hence, their success in achieving their objectives depends on influencing political institutions to adopt the policies and measures they advocate. This may involve securing the attention of political influentials, which may entail using the media to win public sympathy for the case advocated. Even so, it must be stressed that the bulk of pressure group activity is very undramatic and routine, and is invisible to the public eye. It involves a series of detailed discussions with civil servants, MPs or peers about the content and implementation of legislation.

It should also be remembered that pressure groups spend a lot of time talking to other pressure groups. Sometimes this may be to try and build a coalition on a particular issue and thus strengthen a particular case being put to government. More often, however, producer pressure groups are engaged in discussions with other groups with whom they are potentially in conflict. A trade association will usually have more or less formal arrangements for maintaining contacts with its suppliers and its customers. To give an example of one area in which there has been considerable tension: as a small number of supermarket chains have gained an increasing share of grocery sales, the economic power of food manufacturers has diminished relative to that of retailers. This changing balance of power has been reflected in the ability of retailers to demand very large discounts from manufacturers, and in other problems such as lorries from manufacturers having to queue to unload at supermarkets. (For a broader discussion of these problems, see Farago 1987.) Discussions on these problems have taken place on a regular basis between associations representing processors and retailers. These direct contacts do not involve what was defined earlier as the public policy function of government, but a public policy dimension has been introduced when the manufacturers have been successful in getting the issue reviewed by the Monopolies and Mergers Commission.

There is no one route by which pressure groups exert influence. The general features of the process can, however, be presented in the form of a simplified flow diagram (see Figure 3.1). Not all the stages presented in the diagram will be relevant to every instance of a pressure group exerting influence. For example, some cause groups can obtain their objectives through the passage of a private member's bill, such as abortion law reform, the abolition of capital punishment, or (as yet not achieved) the abolition of hunting. A detailed consideration of this particular type of cause group will be presented in the next chapter. However, many cause groups are as concerned to influence government as they are Parliament, for all insider groups issues will usually be pursued first through discussions with ministers and civil servants.

## Getting issues on the political agenda

The political agenda is crowded, and there are limits to the number of issues which can be processed at any one time. This is reflected in the pressures on parliamentary time. Even under the Thatcher Government, which is committed to rolling back the influence of the state, each Queen's Speech contains a substantial amount of new legislation. The Cabinet and its Legislative Committee have to discuss which possible measures are to have priority in a particular session. During the year, there will have to be discussions about whether to offer minor concessions to speed up the passage of a particular piece of legislation, and when and where the 'guillotine' should be applied.

However, important though the legislative agenda is, the political agenda is a somewhat broader concept. It refers to those issues which arouse public concern at a particular period of time. There may be short-run variations in response to particular events, but there may also be longer-term shifts in public opinion. The media undoubtedly plays an

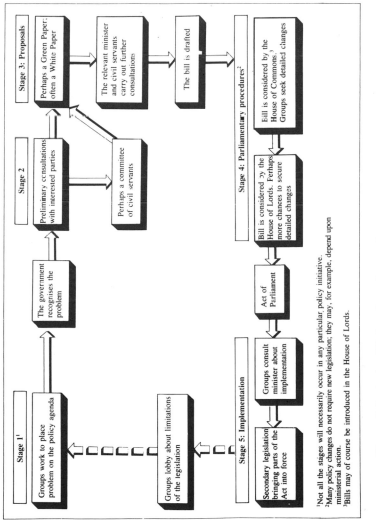

[1]Not all the stages will necessarily occur in any particular policy initiative.
[2]Many policy changes do not require new legislation; they may, for example, depend upon ministerial action.
[3]Bills may of course be introduced in the House of Lords.

**Figure 3.1** A simplified outline of group involvement in the policy process

important role, if not in creating public opinion then at least in reinforcing it. The rise in the importance of the environment as a political issue undoubtedly owed something to increased media attention. In part, this reflected the growth of television as a communications medium, particularly the introduction of colour television. Pollution disasters offer powerful visual images: a spreading oil slick; stunted trees; dying seals.

Some groups, particularly cause groups, may be seeking to establish 'their' issue on the political agenda (or to give it a higher priority) as a prelude to obtaining effective political action. Indeed, the emergence of a new issue may often involve the formation of new cause groups or coalitions of such groups (see the case study of food additives below). Some sectional groups may also wish to obtain public attention for their problems, for example teachers' organisations may wish to draw attention to problems of violence against teachers, or of increasing stress levels being experienced by school heads. Very often, however, sectional groups will want to keep issues away from public attention as much as possible, so that they can be processed through familiar consultative channels. Once an issue has been placed on the political agenda it 'passes into the relatively closed world of the executive departments of state and, to a lesser extent, interdepartmental and cabinet committees, where the consideration given to issues and possible responses by politicians and officials is largely shielded from public gaze' (Solesbury 1976, p. 392). Media attention may soon switch elsewhere and, as Solesbury points out, there are a variety of 'partial responses' open to government which may reassure the public without eradicating the original problem (p. 394).

The 1970s and 1980s have seen the proliferation of private 'think tanks' in Britain which produce policy ideas for consideration by political parties and ministers. The Institute of Economic Affairs, founded in 1957, is thought to have had a significant influence on the way in which the intellectual climate has changed from favouring interventionist, neo-Keynesian ideas to more market-orientated approaches. Margaret Thatcher was among the founders of the Centre for Policy Studies set up after the Conservative defeat in the February 1974 election. The Adam Smith Institute, set up in the USA in 1978 and Britain in 1981, has been the original source of many of the Thatcher Government's policy initiatives, such as Norman Fowler's proposals for privatising NHS ancillary services (see *Labour Research*, February 1984). Although the 'new right' made the running in the organisation of think tanks, organisations linked to the centre and the centre-left have also been formed in the 1980s.

## Food additives: a case study of issue emergence

This case study explores through an examination of food additives the way in which new issues emerge on the political agenda. It is not concerned with the issue of food additives as such, but with the process of issue formation. As background it is, however, necessary to mention briefly the main uses of additives in food manufacturing:

1. Preservatives help food to keep longer. Without them, wastage rates would be higher, and the range of goods that could be stocked would be more limited.
2. Emulsifiers are used to mix together ingredients which would normally separate, for example mayonnaise and salad cream could not be made without an emulsifier. Stabilisers prevent ingredients from separating again.
3. Flavourings are by far the largest category of additives, but they are used in tiny quantities and are rarely entirely artificial. More controversial are flavour enhancers which make existing flavours in the food seem stronger. Monosodium glutamate, which has been widely used, stimulates the taste buds.
4. Artificial colours are another controversial set of additives, particularly tartrazine (E102) which is one of the commonest and has been linked with some adverse reactions.

Everything we know about the environmental and consumer movement suggests that it draws it strongest support from middle- and upper-class groups, and this general conclusion is supported in the particular case of food additives by a study carried out by MAFF. Respondents in the AB and C1 social classes were more likely to name food additives as damaging to health than those in the C2 and DE groupings, although it should be noted that age differences were an even stronger differentiator on this question (with the 55+ age group taking a much more benign view of food additives than those aged between 25 and 34) (MAFF 1987).

The MAFF study underlines the importance of media publicity in relation to issue emergence. Fifty-nine per cent of the women interviewed were aware of recent publicity on the subject, 65 per cent remembering it as part of a television programme (p. 24). A series of structured discussions with six groups of different social compositions showed that 'Most knowledge was media led and so was highly dependent on issues which happened to be taken up, perhaps solely for their news value' (p. 24). Respondents could recall a number of items from television programmes such as *The Food Programme*, but 'Women's magazines and newspapers were also influential . . . via their regular coverage of nutrition, diet and additives' (p. 45). This media interest in the subject had, however, been fostered by a number of books such as Erik Millstone's *Food Additives* and Cannon's *The Politics of Food*. Some respondents in the MAFF study had read *E for Additives*, written by Maurice Hansen, a leader of both British and European associations for health food manufacturers.

## The emergence of new campaigning organisations

At the centre of any map of the new cause groups concerning themselves with food additives stands the London Food Commission (LFC). This body was originally established under the auspices of the GLC (recalling the new socialist approach to pressure group activity at the local authority level referred to in Chapter 2). After the GLC was abolished, it received funding from a trust which outlived the council's demise. The LFC has operated with a small staff, contracting researchers to prepare reports. These are often well prepared, if written from a particular perspective, and attract considerable media attention, with newspapers often referring to the 'independent' LFC.

Although the LFC has attracted attention as a specialist organisation concerned with food policy questions, the broad spectrum of organisations interested in such issues was reflected in the formation in December 1985 of FACT (Food Additives Campaign Team). This is an interesting example of coalition building between pressure groups of the kind referred to at the beginning of the chapter. An introductory statement issued in June 1986 claimed that:

> the widespread use of additives is now a menace to public health. Most additives are the means whereby low quality ingredients, saturated fats and sugars, can be disguised as good nutritious food. Many common additives cause a number of illnesses in vulnerable people, notably children.

The twenty-nine organisations belonging to FACT may be broken down into six categories:

1. Specialist campaigning organisations concerned with food policy issues, such as the London Food Commission, the London Hazards Centre (which has funded LFC research), and the Food Additives Petition.
2. Organisations concerned with particular medical conditions, or

categories of medical condition, or representing paramedical workers. This was the largest single category, including thirteen organisations such as Action Against Allergy, Coronary Prevention Group, Health Visitors' Association, Hyperactive Children's Support Group, and National Eczema Society.

3. Unions concerned with the food industry such as the Bakers, Food and Allied Workers Union and the Transport and General Workers Union.
4. 'Green' organisations such as Friends of the Earth and the Vegetarian Society.
5. Women's organisations such as the National Council of Women of Great Britain and the National Federation of Women's Institutes.
6. General campaigning organisations such as the British Society for Social Responsibility in Science and the Campaign for Freedom of Information.

One group of professionals who have taken a close interest in food additives issues includes persons who work in paramedical occupations (such as dieticians) or who have a paramedical role in a local authority (such as environmental health). Many of these professionals are involved in a new organisation called the Public Health Alliance which was launched in the summer of 1987 at a conference in Birmingham on 'Rethinking Public Health' and has been operating from the offices of the Health Visitors' Association. Press publicity for the conference was organised by the London Borough of Lambeth, and the conference was sponsored by a number of London and metropolitan borough councils, as well as by the Association of Metropolitan Authorities, reflecting the way in which councils saw the formation of new campaigning organisations as one of their functions. The leader of the alliance is Dr David Player, formerly Director-General of the now closed Health Education Council. He saw the task of the Public Health Alliance as being 'to expose and make clear the relationships (and ethics) between interests of MPs and others in authority to forces which are antagonistic to health such as the tobacco industry, alcohol industry, and parts of the food and pharmaceutical industries' (*The Lancet*, 25 July 1987).

These groups do not have very substantial financial resources, but they are linked together by a network of close personal contacts (key individuals occupy leading roles in more than one organisation). The net was cast wider in a third organisation formed in 1988, the National Food Alliance, which brought in the National Farmers' Union and Oxfam alongside the LFC and trade unions. Not surprisingly, it was admitted that 'There's a great sense in the group of the fragility of the alliance. The task is to overcome the suspicions in the group' (*New Society*, 13 May 1988).

Much of the impact enjoyed by the new campaigning groups on food policy has come from their access to the media, and their ability to influence both public opinion and decision makers. However, media publicity of itself would have produced less reaction in the absence of general public concern about the issue. In part, this seems to have been triggered off by the provision of E number information on labels, leading to the widespread belief that 'the E number system identifies ingredients to be avoided' (MAFF 1987, p. 24). The MAFF research also showed that 'Attitudinally, manufacturers were now rarely trusted, because they were seen as, or suspected to exert little control and "conscience" over their use of additives' (p. 39). Retailers were regarded as having taken more positive steps to aid consumers, both by providing information and by stocking additive-free products. It was also clear that there was a great deal of folklore circulating about hyperactive children, and that food additives are regularly seized upon as an explanation of bad behaviour. For example, one participant in the group discussions for the MAFF survey commented, 'I have a neighbour whose little boy was always playing up and their doctor said it was that thing in orange squashes and he's much better now.'

## The response of established sectoral groups

The campaigning organisations concerned with food additives have succeeded in getting the issue on to the public agenda, although the process for approving additives has not changed as a result. Sectional groups concerned with food additives have, however, had to respond to the criticisms. The Food and Drink Federation:

> does not consider that the food industry should assume *direct* responsibility for the nutritional status of the population. It believes that the role of these industries is to make available the widest possible range of foodstuffs manufactured and labelled in compliance with the law, and in accordance with the principles of good manufacturing practice.
> 
> (Stocker 1985, p. 13)

One response that is available to the food manufacturing industry is, of course, to use the fact that particular products are 'additive-free' or use 'no artificial additives'. In many respects, the greatest potential impact of the issue is on chemical firms who manufacture food additives. These firms are organised in the Food Sector Group of the Chemical Industries Association. They have published a booklet called *The Chemistry on Your Table* in response to criticisms of food additives, and have placed greater emphasis on contacts with the media.

## Lessons from the case study

A number of general lessons can be drawn from this case study:

1. In order for an issue to gain higher prominence, there has to be some underlying public concern or interest in the first place.
2. This public concern can be focused and intensified by the media.
3. The emergence of an issue is often associated with the formation of new cause groups, or of alliances of existing groups (which may be both cause and sectional).
4. Existing sectional groups will have to respond to the emergence of the issue on the agenda, perhaps by extending the range of their activities in relation to the media.
5. Issue emergence should not be confused with the achievement of a shift in policy, although getting the issue on the policy agenda is the first step towards that goal. In the particular case discussed, the new groups remained outsider groups, and the decision-making processes on food additives did not change. Indeed, MAFF produced a booklet advertised on television called *Food Additives: The Balanced Approach*, which argued that 'The negative side of additives has been given publicity.'

## Influencing the executive branch of government

The Devlin Commission on Industrial Representation argued that 'All executive policy and most legislation is conceived, framed, drafted and all but enacted in Whitehall' (Devlin Commission 1972, p. 5). This statement was an exaggeration when it was made; moreover, Parliament has probably acquired greater influence since it was made. Even so, it contains a substantial element of truth. As a senior official of the National Farmers' Union has commented:

Getting in early is a very important golden rule. We have a sort of intelligence role on behalf of the farmers to keep our ears to the ground to find out what new initiatives are being proposed and what legislation may be coming on with the object of influencing it from the outset ... Whatever it is we shall be wanting to take an interest from the earliest stage. There is no question that once a piece of legislation reaches Parliament you may be able to tinker around the edges, but the prospect of getting any significant changes at that stage are very remote indeed ... Therefore it makes it much more important to try to get it right before it ever enters Parliament.

(Holbeche 1986, p. 46)

Insider groups will try to influence policy when it is at the formative stage by talking informally to civil servants and ministers. In this respect, membership of some of the large number of advisory committees maintained by government may be important. As Jordan and Richardson observe (1987, p. 185), 'Through regularized participation in these structures, groups are able to shape the definition and perception of problems, influence the political agenda in those policy areas of direct concern to them, and influence the perception and emergence of "practicable" solutions.' The more solidified the proposal becomes, the more difficult it is to change. Even once a (consultative) Green Paper has been published, there are limits to the extent to which government will be prepared to modify its policies; this is even more true in the case of a White Paper, which can be seen as a statement of the government's intentions. Of course, consultations will go on in between the publication of the White Paper and the presentation of a bill to Parliament. However, by this stage they will be increasingly formal and even ritualistic, and the government's room for manœuvre without losing face will be seriously limited. As Bruce-Gardyne (1986, p. 152) explains in the light of his experience as a minister:

the safest solution for the corporate lobbyist is to fix his trade association, and then to watch his trade association fix the civil service. For once the deal is done, the honour of the civil service is engaged. If it then fails to deliver its Ministers bound hand and foot, it hangs its head in shame. Whereas the lobby which converts the politicians is inevitably confronted by the resistance of the civil service.

## The structure of government

In understanding how insider groups influence policy at the formative stage, it is really necessary to start with the structure of government itself. Policy communities tend to form around government departments, and pressure groups are often concerned when departments are reorganised. For example, the roads lobby was unhappy when the Ministry of Transport was incorporated into the Department of the Environment in 1970. In 1976 a new Department of Transport was created. 'The experience of the DoE suggested that the transport community was not happy to form part of an integrated land-use planning department, and possessed the political power to withstand this assault from those campaigning for greater integration' (Dudley 1983, p. 113).

Although most insider pressure groups will have contacts with a range of departments, they tend to have particularly close contacts with one department. Indeed, they may encounter difficulties in establishing relations with departments with which they are not familiar. This is partly because each department is anxious to defend its clients, for example the Energy Department has tended to defend interests of energy-producing industries against energy users. It is also a reflection of the importance of 'departmentalism' within the culture of the British civil service. 'The distinctive culture of the department is at least as important as the culture of Whitehall as a whole' (Plowden 1985, p. 26). Whiteley and Winyard (1987, p. 94) noted the existence of different 'house-styles' and bureaucratic cultures from department to department, while a study of the chemical industry found considerable differences in departmental attitudes towards the industry (Grant, Paterson and Whitston 1988).

It is also important to take account of the relative importance attached to different functions within a department. Discussing the organisation of the Ministry of Agriculture, Fisheries and Food (in the immediate post-war period, there was a distinct Ministry of Food), a senior official of a food-processing industry association has commented:

> All Ministers at Whitehall Place do from time to time assure the food industry of their awareness that they are ministers of Food *too* but in recent times they have in reality been, according to party, an extension of Ministers of Consumer Affairs or simply Ministers of Agriculture and, perhaps, fisheries. Their policies have, it is true, sometimes been of benefit to this or that part of the food industry but that has been almost entirely coincidental.
>
> (Stocker 1983, pp. 250–1)

Some interest groups may have a close relationship with a particular junior minister who is perceived as an advocate for their particular needs; indeed, they may have lobbied for the particular post to be established. Examples include the creation of a post of Minister for the Arts in 1964 (probably most successful as a means of promoting the arts under its first incumbent, Jenny Lee) and a Minister for the Disabled in 1974. Although the effectiveness of such ministers has sometimes been questioned, Theakston (1987, p. 161) points to 'the increased expenditure secured through their championing of their clients; their liaison work with organizations at arm's length from Whitehall, local authorities and interest groups, helping keep the government in touch with problems and views outside; and the consolidation of responsibilities within Whitehall achieved under them'.

## The role of sponsorship divisions

For much of the post-war period, the relationship between government and industry in particular was organised through sponsorship divisions, located principally within the Department of Trade and Industry (in its various forms), but also elsewhere in government. Every product, ranging from aerial ropeways, through diamonds, fireworks and musical instruments, to wreck clearance, had a departmental sponsor somewhere in government. The sponsoring divisions were thus the first port of call for trade associations. In turn, the sponsoring divisions acted as 'institutionalised trade associations' within government, raising issues that concerned their industry with other departments, and also offering trade associations general advice on their relationships with government. However, as well as looking after the interests of particular industries within government, the sponsorship divisions were also responsible for explaining government policies to their industries. They were thus involved in a two-way flow of information between industry and government.

In January 1988 it was announced that sponsorship divisions were being abolished in the Department of Trade and Industry (although they were being retained in other government departments such as MAFF, the Department of Health and Social Security, and the Scottish Office). The White Paper making the announcement argued that 'It is in nobody's interests for DTI to be an uncritical spokesman in Whitehall for business interests. The change from industry to market divisions will help ensure that does not occur' (Cm. 278 1988, p. 39). Lord Young, the Secretary of State for Trade and Industry, made it clear that he intended to foster direct contacts with managers, by-passing the traditional route of contact through trade associations. He described associations as 'the lowest common denominator, producing mutual dependency between sectors and sponsoring civil servants' (*Financial Times*, 16 January 1988).

Part of the thinking behind these changes was that the DTI was too close to industry, that it was taking the side of industry without thinking what was an objective point of view (although, in practice, civil servants in sponsorship divisions had always placed representations from trade associations within the context of government policy). The new arrangements envisaged more direct contact with individual companies, with the DTI's London offices handling relations with large companies, and an expanded network of regional offices dealing with medium-sized and smaller companies. Such an approach to government—industry relations has been characterised as a 'company state' format, in contrast to notions of the 'corporate state' (Willis and Grant 1987).

Trade associations have not been entirely sidelined in the new arrangements, but the latter enable the department to take a more selective approach to the associations, which they view as variable in quality. In particular, associations will still be used as a means of bringing companies together and explaining developments in government policy. It is apparent, however, that the representative significance of trade associations has been downgraded. This has resulted not from any change in the resources or strategies of the associations, but from a shift in government policy.

This particular development is not only important in itself (business associations are the numerically largest category of pressure group), but also emphasises the extent to which government influences the form and pattern of pressure group activity. A comparative study of the organisation of business associations in the construction industry in Britain and West Germany found that there was a close correspondence between the division of representation between various associations and the form of organisation of the machinery of government in the two countries (Grant and Streeck 1985). Moreover, government can be an important source of funds. Of the environmental groups studied by Lowe and Goyder (1983, p. 42), '23 per cent are heavily dependent on government as their first or second most important source of income'. Similarly, of the poverty lobby groups studied by Whiteley and Winyard (1987, p. 29), 'The government is an important source of funds, used to varying degrees by over three-quarters (thirty-three) of the groups.' Whiteley and Winyard found that the receipt of government money did not in general inhibit the groups, although the Director of MIND was obliged to apologise for accusations of brutality in secure pyschiatric hospitals after the Secretary of State made it clear that the organisation might lose some or all of its grant (p. 30).

## The dullness of lobbying

It has to be emphasised that most lobbying is a rather dull business carried on between two sets of bureaucrats. Pressure groups employ professional staff, usually structured on relatively hierarchical lines. They then go and engage in detailed discussions with other bureaucrats working for the civil service about the details of, for example, a statutory instrument implementing an EC directive. As Miller stresses, much of what goes on is 'the legalistic negotiation of a case with rather dull junior to middle ranking officials in rather dull Whitehall offices' (Miller 1988, not paginated).

Most representations, in fact, should be directed at a relatively low level of the administrative hierarchy. As one under-secretary is reported as commenting, 'Action is taken at the lowest level in the Civil Service at which it can be competently handled' (Public Policy Consultants 1987, p. 16). Busy permanent or deputy secretaries are not usually going to contradict the advice given to them by junior officials who know much more about the issue under consideration. A booklet on working with Whitehall prepared for the CBI notes, 'it is the senior executive officer or higher executive officer in charge of a section of a policy division whose work is most likely to be relevant to the businessman' (Coffin 1987, p. 32). Whether such advice is taken is another matter; Public Policy Consultants (1987, p. 15) found that 77 per cent of the ministers and officials in their sample thought that pressure groups suffered from a mistaken desire to take things to the top.

The frequency of contact will vary from one group to another. Whiteley and Winyard (1987, pp. 92–3) make a distinction between regular, periodical and infrequent contacts, ranging from day-to-day relations to a major meeting once a year. Similar distinctions would apply to sectional groups. However, it should be noted that a particular issue may lead to more intensive contacts than usual. For example, the Ice Cream Federation had more than its usual level of contact with MAFF while an EC directive on ice cream was under consideration.

The process of consultation usually starts with the department sending out a proposal for comment to a range of groups. For example, in 1985 the Government sent out a 99-page consultative document on a review of food law (see Figure 3.2). Lists are maintained for the purposes of circulating such documents; they are usually rather long (that maintained by MAFF for food policy matters contains the names of seventy-seven associations). The civil service considers that it is better to over-consult than to under-consult. As one senior civil servant has commented:

> We consult on any proposal those organisations which seem to be
> representative of the subject or interests under discussion. It is a subjective
> judgement on every occasion but we work on the basis that we would
> sooner over-consult rather than under-consult because you cannot from
> our position judge the importance on occasions of a particular proposal
> to a particular group of people.
>
> (Quoted in Coates 1984, pp. 146–7)

It is not anticipated that all, or even a majority, of associations will
respond to proposals circulated by the ministry. For example, in the case
of the EC's proposed jams directive, the Commission's proposals were
sent out to about 100 organisations for comment. Twenty-four replied,

---

1. The Government has decided to publish this consultative document
following the announcement of a review of food legislation which was
made in November 1983. The purpose of this document is to review
the areas where some change in the primary food legislation may be
desirable, to stimulate discussion and to invite comments from interested
parties. The Government will decide what further action is needed in
the light of comments received.

2. This document deals with the United Kingdom as a whole, although
there are at present three separate Acts: in England and Wales the Food
Act 1984, in Scotland the Food and Drugs Act (Scotland) 1956 and
in Northern Ireland the Food and Drugs Act (Northern Ireland) 1958.
The document only refers to those sections of the Acts (hereafter
referred to as the 1984, 1956 and 1958 Acts) for which the main changes
are proposed and it is recognised that there are likely to be many other
useful amendments which could be made. Comments will be welcome
on any matter relevant to the Acts, whether or not they are mentioned
in the document.

3. Written comments should as far as possible follow the framework of
the recommendations made. They should be sent by 1 June 1985 in
England and Wales to Standards Division, MAFF, Room 432, Great
Westminster House, Horseferry Road, London SW1P 2AE; in Scotland
to Foods Branch, SHHD, Room 42, St Andrews House, Edinburgh
EH2 3DE; or in Northern Ireland to Medicines and Food Control
Branch, DHSS, Annex A, Dundonald House, Belfast BT4 3SF. When
these submissions have been examined officials will be pleased to
discuss points of particular interest with the main representative
organisations.

---

**Figure 3.2**   Preface to the review of food legislation: consultative document

of which six did not offer any substantive comments. Apart from a special meeting with the Cake and Biscuit Alliance on the special problem of bakery jam, the principal meetings were with the Preserves Section of the Food Manufacturers' Federation, which also received reports by letter on each meeting of the Council of Ministers working group (Coates 1984, pp. 152−3).

The initial consultation process could be viewed as a trawling exercise in which not everything that is obtained will be of value. A further process of sifting and grading has to follow. Most of the meetings that take place will be between pressure group representatives and civil servants, although occasionally ministers will become directly involved. The result will often be a rather formal, 'set piece' affair in which both sides state their positions. Indeed, one of the chores given to junior ministers is to 'receive a large number of deputations and delegations to save them going to the top minister' (Theakston 1987, p. 139). Sometimes such meetings seem to be held for the benefit of the vanity of the pressure group's members. One experienced director of a regionally based association told me after his retirement that his members were great believers in delegations to London. He recalled, 'They would put their case bluntly to the minister − with little effect − and the man from the *Yorkshire Post* would be waiting outside the building and they would say, "We told him!" '

The annual 'Budget representations', made by a variety of associations to the Chancellor, often seem to have a rather ritualistic character. The Chancellor is faced with a wide variety of proposals. In the run-up to the 1989 Budget, the Chancellor was confronted by a campaign calling for the zero-rating of human food to be extended to pet food. The campaign was headed by the Pet Food Manufacturers' Association, backed up by an alliance of slaughterhouse owners, vets, animal charities, pensioners' pressure groups, dog and cat breeders and bird fanciers, claiming to represent eighteen million dogs, cats, budgies and fish (*Independent*, 29 November 1988). The annual rituals of budgetary lobbying, with their stock phrases and procedures, are amusingly recalled by Bruce-Gardyne (1986, pp. 157−9). He suspects that often the whole exercise is for the benefit of the trade press photographer waiting on the Treasury doorstep. The delegation is duly displayed 'to advantage over a story reporting that they have "made the strongest representations" and "received a sympathetic hearing" ' (p. 159).

Even so, there are times when it is useful to involve the minister; often it may be more appropriate to approach a junior minister who is handling a particular area of policy. For all the constraints and limitations that they face, 'It is indisputable that in the 1970s and 1980s junior ministers in general have played more significant roles and carried more weight in Westminster and Whitehall than in the 1940, 1950s and early 1960s (Theakston 1987, p. 79). More generally, as Whiteley and Winyard note (1983, p. 93), 'the view that civil servants run things and that the minister has to go along with this is an over-simplification. Individual ministers were perceived to make a real difference to outcomes.' Some key decisions, such as whether to refer a proposed takeover bid to the Monopolies and Mergers Commission, ultimately have to be made by the minister personally, albeit on the basis of advice offered by his civil servants. Such decisions are generally taken in the political limelight, with the political and media spotlight on the minister.

It must also be emphasised that some contacts take place at a very high level within government, particularly when major companies are involved. For example, when ICI was worried about a change in tax law which it thought would adversely affect its operations, meetings took place between the Chairman of ICI and the then Chancellor of the Exchequer, the Chief Secretary of the Treasury, and other ministers and senior officials of the Inland Revenue. It is not unknown for chairmen and managing directors of major companies to have meetings at prime ministerial level.

## Policy implementation and enforcement

The consideration of policy implementation and enforcement really belongs to a discussion of relationships between pressure groups and the executive branch of government, even though Parliament has a role in the passage of delegated legislation. Many Acts of Parliament 'require secondary legislation in order to set out powers, rights and duties in detail. A considerable proportion of primary legislation now empowers Departments to formulate Regulations that provide this detail in a way that would be inappropriate for inclusion in the body of the Act itself' (Miller 1987, pp. 71–2). In effect, there is an increasing use of enabling legislation which transfers to the minister the right to make specific regulations. Parliamentary scrutiny of such regulations is limited in its effect. Less than a quarter of the 2,500 or so statutory instruments made each year are referred to a Select Committee, 'whose duty is to scrutinize them under very restricted terms of reference' (Taylor 1979, p. 131).

Sectional pressure groups are understandably very interested in the contents of statutory instruments. Detailed variations may influence considerably the activities and financial rewards of their members. The CBI, for example, found it useful to publish a guide for its members 'to the myriad statutory instruments made under the Control of Pollution Act' (CBI Annual Report 1984, p. 13). When it comes to exerting influence on the content of ministerial regulations, detailed discussions will take place between civil servants and pressure group officials. For example, the Chemical Industries Association (CIA) noted in its 1986 activities report in relation to legislation on the control of substances hazardous to health:

> Revised proposals for regulations are likely to appear in Autumn 1986 and will be significantly changed as a result of the representations led by the Chemical Industry Health Safety and Environment Council. In particular our statements and public representations drew attention to the unnecessary complexity and over-ambitious nature of the proposals in the first consultative document.

Pressure groups may also collaborate with government in drawing up guidance on how regulations are to be interpreted and implemented. Thus, for example, the Chlorine Group of the CIA collaborated with the Health and Safety Executive in the production of a document called *Best Practical Means for Chemical Works*. The CIA's Isocyanates Product Group collaborated with the Health and Safety Executive and the International Isocyanate Institute on the measurement of toluene diisocyanate to enable users to comply with the HSE's new limits for the product. The fact that such matters are highly technical does not mean that they are unimportant in terms of either the impact on particular companies or more general public policy considerations.

It is also important to consider the way in which laws and regulations are enforced. For example, food law in Britain is enforced largely at the retail rather than the production level. There are provisions in the legislation for enforcement officers to enter factories, but they are rarely used. There is pressure from the European Community for representative sampling of products in the factory or warehouse. Reviewing the matter, MAFF stresses that it is very difficult to see how such changes could be introduced 'except on a very long term scale and with agreement by interested parties' (MAFF 1985, p. 49). 'In fact, in view of the complexities of the subject no general move away from the present point of enforcement could be recommended without more debate amongst all interested parties (p. 50).

## The benefits of being on the inside track

It is apparent from the evidence reviewed in this chapter that there are extensive contacts between pressure groups and the executive branches of government during the development of policy and its implementation. If anything, the growing importance of EC decisions has increased the importance of such contacts. Many decisions are clearly taken within relatively closed policy communities in which the complexity of the problems being discussed often constitutes a significant entry barrier. Thus, in his discussion of food standards, Coates (1984, p. 157) observes that:

> Possible changes are widely canvassed, thoroughly discussed, considered in detail and, if broadly acceptable to all who show an interest, put into effect ... This continuous process of consultation tends to commit the whole policy community not only to the policy process but also the decisions it brings forth ... almost all members of the policy community have an interest in the smooth functioning of the system.

Consider the values that are embedded in that statement. The first is that of extensive and detailed consultation. The second is that of acceptability to affected interests. A third is the commitment of pressure groups to decisions arrived at through the process of consultation. A fourth is the assumption that both government and groups have an interest in continuity and stability in the policy process. These values might be summarised as the 'four Cs' of insider pressure group politics:

1. *consultation* with recognised interests
2. *consent* by the interest groups consulted to the decisions taken by government
3. *co-operation* by the groups in the implementation of the decisions
4. *continuity* in the contours of the policy-making process.

Such a policy process tends to benefit insider groups. As Miller (1987, p. 98) remarks:

> It has often been commented that Departments predominantly represent single interests ... While that is a sweeping generalization, it is frequently the case that non-Establishment pressure groups such as Friends of the Earth find it difficult to obtain equal billing with interests sponsored by officials. Pressure groups are called just that because officials prefer to maintain the status quo rather than involve their Department — and possibly a number of others — in the time, expense and disruption of revising policy or initiating legislation unless they feel it to be absolutely necessary.

Alternative channels are available to groups lacking insider status, through using the media to establish their concerns on the policy agenda, through the courts, or through the passage of private members' bills in Parliament. These methods will be considered in the next chapter. Miller (pp. 56–9) from his vantage point as Chief Executive of Public Policy Consultants assigns influence scores to various components of the political system. The prime minister receives a score of ten out of ten; officials eight; and ministers seven. Apart from the whips, the highest score given to a parliamentary body is six for the House of Lords EEC Committee; MPs/peers as a group receive four, rising to six if there is a small majority or a very public or political issue. Access to decision makers in the executive branch clearly has its advantages.

# 4

# Exerting Pressure Outside Whitehall

This chapter is concerned with pressure group activity away from Whitehall: in Parliament, through the use of the media, in the courts, and in local government. These routes are particularly used by 'outsider' groups who lack good contacts with civil servants, but they are certainly not neglected by 'insider' groups. For a variety of reasons, they have tended to be used increasingly over time.

## Parliament

Jordan and Richardson (1987, p. 252) observe that 'Parliamentary activity is perhaps particularly important for environmental, social issue, and other cause groups without good connections to Whitehall and the civil service'. As will be seen later, cause groups can often attain their objectives through the passage of a private member's bill. However, sectional groups can also make effective use of parliamentary contacts. Bruce-Gardyne (1986, pp. 152−3) recalls what happened when, as a minister, he was presented with a complex scheme designed to enable horse traders to escape VAT:

> I was vastly unimpressed, until I was accosted by one of my senior colleagues in the corridors of Westminster. 'I hear', he told me in a voice full of menace, 'that you're being bloody-minded about our horse-trading scheme. Well forget it. It was all fixed up with your predecessor, and

I can assure you that if you muck it around, we'll make your life a misery.'
I had second thoughts.

For the greater part of the 1974–9 Parliament, the Government lacked a majority, and this encouraged sectional groups to make greater use of contacts with Parliament to modify or overturn decisions. The CBI, for example, set up a parliamentary unit in 1977, developing a lobbying system based on that of the National Farmers' Union, with links at the constituency level between industrialists and their MPs. At Westminister, the CBI 'wooed the smallest parties' (MacDougall 1987, p. 232). The Scottish Nationalists were invited to CBI headquarters for a working dinner and 'were subsequently helpful on several occasions by casting their votes in the way we wanted' (p. 233).

Most associations representing particular industries will either have their own small staff dealing with Parliament, or retain a firm of parliamentary lobbyists to assist them with parliamentary representation. For example, the Chemical Industries Association employs a Parliamentary Adviser, and administers the All Party Parliamentary Group for the Chemical Industry with a membership of some seventy MPs together with members of the House of Lords. The group meets to hear about developments in the industry and to discuss relevant legislation, and its members are also individually briefed on a large number of subjects. A piece of legislation which is particularly important to the CIA may involve the Parliamentary Adviser attending every debate and committee session in the Commons and Lords; briefing individual committee members, civil servants and ministers; and commenting on large numbers of amendments put down by MPs.

## Ways of using Parliament

Parliament is made up of two houses; a variety of mechanisms for processing legislation and discussing current political issues; and (counting active peers) over a thousand individuals with a wide variety of political interests and priorities. How can pressure groups go about influencing a very complex institution which is understandably protective of its traditions and privileges?

One possibility is to organise a letter-writing campaign. Certainly, MPs are receiving more and more letters: one source has estimated that they were receiving twice as many letters in 1987 as they were seven years earlier (Public Policy Consultants 1987, p. 9). Many of these letters will, of course, be concerned with problems faced by individual constituents, and MPs will give consideration of such letters a high priority. Circulars from pressure groups are likely to receive little, if any, attention unless the MP or peer has a special interest in the issue. Several MPs responding to one questionnaire commented that 'the House of Commons has the biggest waste paper bins in the country and it was a common admission that at least 50 per cent of MPs' mail goes straight to the bin, much of it unopened' (p. 17).

One tactic that a pressure group may use to avoid the waste-paper basket is to get its members to write to their MP on an issue which concerns it. Such a stratagem can backfire if it is not well managed. Bruce-Gardyne recalls that MPs received a large number of letters in 1980 from Catholic constituents complaining about a plan to charge for school transport. 'On closer inspection most of these communications had fairly obviously been signed, not by Catholic voters at all, but by their children scribbling under the vigilant eye of their local parish priests' (Bruce-Gardyne 1986, p. 155). Far more effective was a lobby against new controls on shotgun ownership based on handwritten letters from the chairmen of village Conservative branches (p. 155).

MPs may be wined and dined to make them sympathetic to a particular point of view. Over two-thirds of those questioned by Public Policy Consultants thought that 'entertainment as a lobbying medium is over-used and under-exploited when it is used' (Public Policy Consultants 1987, p. 25). All the ministers interviewed 'claimed that they would discount representations from MPs retained by organisations on whose behalf they were lobbying' (p. 27). Nevertheless, many organisations and companies (including, of course, trade unions) do retain MPs and peers.

What are they getting for their money, apart from the ability to dine important clients at Westminster, or to arrange meetings there (actually quite important motivations)? An MP or peer can, of course, put down a question as a means of obtaining information about government policy, although a pressure group with good civil service contacts should be able to obtain that anyway. However, in the case of oral questions it may sometimes be possible to embarrass the government into action through probing supplementaries. The MP or peer can raise matters through adjournment debates or, in the Lords, through the device of the Unstarred Question (which leads to a debate). Early Day Motions (that is, motions that in practice are not debated) can be used to give publicity to a problem, although such motions have arguably been devalued through their over use by professional lobbyists seeking to show their clients some tangible result for their fees. Indeed, there is considerable opposition among MPs and ministers to the increasing use of Parliamentary Questions and Early Day Motions as a lobbying device (p. 22).

There is a particular danger of equating activity with effectiveness in the case of Parliament, and it should be remembered that it is very unusual for a government with a working majority to be defeated on the floor of the House of Commons on one of its bills. It was the absence of a working majority in the 1975−9 period which increased the attention given by pressure groups to influencing MPs; indeed, this attention seems to have outlived its original cause. Occasionally, of course, a government with a majority may be defeated on the floor of the House. This happened in April 1986 when a large-scale Conservative rebellion led to a Government defeat on the Sunday trading bill at second reading stage. Such defeats are rare, however, and most of the rebellions which have been advertised in advance have ended up with the Government suffering the embarrassment of a reduction in its majority, but with the legislation being passed intact.

A more successful strategy may be to change the detailed provisions of a bill in a way which is of benefit to a pressure group's members. An attempt can be made to do this at standing committee stage when the bill is considered line by line − although, of course, standing committees are whipped. There is, however, always the possibility of government backbenchers siding with the opposition to defeat a particular clause which concerns a pressure group. Sometimes they can be bought off with promises of future action, but from time to time the government considers that the best course of action is to make concessions.

## The House of Lords

The House of Lords offers another opportunity to make detailed amendments. If they are too contentious, they are likely to be reversed when the measure returns to the Commons. However, the House of Lords offers fruitful ground for inserting relatively technical amendments which may be important to a pressure group's members. Even if the amendment is not pressed to a vote, it may be used to extract further assurances from the government. This is a tactic which has been used with considerable success by the CBI over the years. When the 1966−70 Labour Government announced its intention to reform the Lords, the CBI stated that it would 'take any opportunity of advocating the retention of arrangements which would preserve the advantages industry has enjoyed under the present system' (CBI Annual Report 1967, p. 22). Indeed, Bruce-Gardyne (1986, p. 147) argues that 'Whitehall remains ill-equipped to handle the House of Lords.' It is not easy to find junior ministers to represent a department in the Lords, and they are then called upon to handle all aspects of its work.

## Private bills

Private bills (not private *members'* bills) constitute a form of legislation which is often of particular interest to sectional pressure groups. Without going into all the complexities of this particular type of legislation (there are also hybrid bills), these are largely bills promoted by local authorities or nationalised industries to acquire land or undertake some new activity. Such a measure was being considered at the time of writing as a means of promoting British Rail's new route to the Channel Tunnel, although it was argued that this was a less appropriate way than a public inquiry to deal with such a complex and contentious proposal. Proposals put forward by Labour-controlled local authorities have sometimes attracted the opposition of bodies such as the CBI. As many as seventy bills of this type may be passed in a parliamentary session. The committee stage of such bills has a quasi-judicial character, with counsel representing both sides, and evidence given on oath. Because of the expense involved, promoters of such measures are generally willing to enter into discussions before committee stage to agree amendments.

## Parliamentary committees

Executive policies and actions are scrutinised by select committees of both Houses. Pressure groups dutifully prepare memoranda of evidence for such bodies, and the more important ones are asked to present themselves to answer questions from committee members. Occasionally, such inquiries may attract considerable public attention, as with the House of Lords investigation into overseas trade in 1984—5. The committee questioned leading industrialists, and what emerged was a report that amounted in large part to a critique of the Government's industrial policy. The Government was almost disproportionately enraged about this affront but, although the hearings and the report aroused a great deal of interest in the quality press, it led to no apparent changes in policy. On the other hand, a critical House of Lords report in 1986—7 on civil research and development prompted a Government reply which did announce important changes in policy. In general, however, the select committees 'produce a constant flow of reports which are rarely discussed in Parliament, and seldom make a stir . . . rarely, in practice, do they make much impact on departmental policies' (Bruce-Gardyne 1986, p. 141). (The Public Accounts Committee is something of an exception, but this is concerned with questioning civil servants and ministers about defects in the execution of policy rather than hearing pressure group representations.)

In many ways, it is reports from House of Lords committees which seem to have had the greatest impact in recent years. This may reflect the fact that the committees often include peers with direct experience of the subject under discussion, and also that they have time to carry out a more thorough inquiry. Mention should also be made of the House of Lords European Communities Committee (which operates through specialist sub-committees). The House of Commons European Legislation Committee simply recommends whether or not Community proposals should be debated, 'whereas the Lords Committees tend to work on subjects rather than documents and can therefore work in advance of the Commission finalizing decisions' (Miller 1987, p. 114).

In practice, some of the most influential bodies in Parliament are the little-known but important specialist backbench committees of MPs interested in a particular subject. Clearly, it is the backbench committees of the governing party that are of real importance; such committees happen to be better developed in the Conservative Party. Miller (p. 42) notes that 'At a time of large Government majorities they are a powerful focus for backbench opinion on the Government side, with privileged access to Ministers and a representative role enhanced by their regular meetings, at which business, industry and other interest groups are given the opportunity to voice their concerns or be questioned by MPs.' Ministers have been persuaded to drop contentious proposals because of a backbench revolt in one of these committees, as happened, for example, with the Thatcher Government's first set of proposals to introduce student loans. Bruce-Gardyne (1986, p. 185) recalls that the officers of the Conservative backbench Finance Committee were regular visitors to the Treasury 'since it is a prime function of the Committee officers in the Tory Party to alert "their" ministers to the waves of Westminster opinion'. Bruce-Gardyne's experience was that their impact was limited by their tendency to disagree with each other more than they disagreed with ministers. Even so, they are an important target for pressure group activity at Westminister.

## Professional lobbyists

The 1980s have seen a considerable proliferation of professional 'lobbyists' offering to act as intermediaries between pressure groups and Parliament (or, for that matter, Whitehall, although Parliament is often their main field of activity). Sectional groups and companies are the main users of their services, although well-resourced cause groups may have their own parliamentary lobbyist. Much of the work of lobbyists often consists of monitoring developments, and drawing the attention of clients to emerging issues which should concern them. Given that they have staff reading Hansard and other parliamentary documents for a number of clients, they are often able to provide such a service more economically than if a pressure group tried to undertake this sifting work for itself. They also build up a body of knowledge about the special interests of MPs, which they can utilise to meet the particular needs of their clients. One consultant explained in interview that the nature of the work:

> Depends on the nature of the lobby, depends on what one's objectives are. There are 101 different things − identifying MPs who are personally interested and sympathetic, briefing people before 2nd Readings in public bills, suggesting amendments, a lot of work during standing committees.

The growth of such professional lobbyists has raised a number of ethical issues, not least about MPs who are directly involved in the running of such companies. Thirty-nine MPs own or are employed by public relations or consultancy firms, with a total of 150 MPs holding 280 consultancies betwen them (Doig 1986, p. 39). There is concern about whether access is being bought, given that the fees of these professional lobbyists are not low. Concern has been expressed that 'the better organised and richer interests will push out the less so' (p. 43). However, it must be noted that, although many consultancy firms are very politically sophisticated and display a high level of professional skill, there is always an element of the 'emperor's clothes' about the work of professional lobbyists. There is never a tangible end product which can be attributed to the efforts of the lobbyist; if the campaign is successful, it may have nothing to do with the lobbyist's efforts. Some less well-informed clients are too easily impressed by lunches being arranged with MPs, or with being escorted to meetings at the Palace of Westminster.

One of the reasons why MPs are sometimes receptive to professional lobbyists is that they are overworked and poorly provided with support staff and facilities. Improvements in this area might help to offset worries about the susceptibility of MPs to external pressures. Even so, as the

House of Commons Select Committee on Members' Interests has stated in a review of the issue, 'It is the right of any citizen to lobby his Member of Parliament, and if he considers that his case can be better advanced with professional assistance he has every right to avail himself of that assistance' (House of Commons 1985, p. iii).

## Private members' bills

Private members' bills offer one route by which pressure groups, particularly cause groups, can hope to attain their objectives. However, it is a hazardous route, even for relatively uncontentious proposals. Relatively few private members' measures ever become law:

> The scales are heavily weighted against them. In the first place the Government takes up most of the time of the House for its own business, so that a Private Member has to be more than fortunate to get enough time to take a Bill through all its stages before the end of the Session. In the second place it is difficult for a Private Member to organize a majority favourable towards his Bill − or, as is more usually the case, to prevent a majority of unfavourable Members voting against it.
>
> (Taylor 1979, p.89)

Capital punishment was abolished, abortion legalised, divorce liberalised and theatre censorship ended through private members' legislation, but the period between 1964 and 1970 was exceptional. Major changes were brought about through private members' legislation during this period 'because the Labour Government granted time to the various bills' (Marsh and Read 1988, p. 64). Far more typical of the successful use of private members' legislation by pressure groups is the relatively technical measure which offends no important countervailing interest. A member who wins a high place on the ballot for private members' bills will receive many approaches from groups who would like him to introduce their proposals as bills. Marsh and Read (pp. 63−4) cite the case of a Conservative MP who having specified 'no animals, no sex' was offered a bill by the British Insurance Brokers Association who wanted to establish a register of legitimate insurance brokers. 'The bill was passed without a vote although there was considerable debate and the Government granted time for the consideration of Lords' amendments' (p. 64).

Abortion is one of the most emotive issues in contemporary politics, and bills designed to restrict the liberalisation introduced by the 1967 Act have become almost an annual feature of the parliamentary calendar.

However, it is difficult to dislodge private members' legislation once it has been passed, and it is therefore important to consider briefly how the original legislation reached the statute book. Founded in 1936, the Abortion Law Reform Association (ALRA) was regarded for many years as 'a morally subversive, crank organisation' (Hindell and Simms 1974, p. 162). In 1963 ALRA leadership positions were taken over by a new group of younger leaders dissatisfied with the organisation's effectiveness. A number of factors contributed to the success of the Steel bill, including the presence of a new wave of liberally minded MPs elected in 1964 and 1966, and what amounted to Government support for reform (see Marsh and Chambers 1981, pp. 17–21). Public opinion was, however, undoubtedly an important factor:

> The abortion lobby became successful when it was able to demonstrate to Parliament that despite religious opposition, public opinion had finally caught up with the views it had been expressing for thirty years. The lobby did not create this opinion, for many factors were at work, but it did influence public opinion, hasten it, and organize it when the time was ripe.
> (Hindell and Simms 1974, p. 163)

The anti-abortion lobby has grown considerably in strength since 1967 (the first anti-abortion group was launched during the passage of the Steel bill), but by 1989 it had not even succeeded in amending, let alone repealing, the 1967 legislation. Defenders of the status quo have the advantage that they can use parliamentary procedure to help to defeat attempts at change. Despite the strength of the anti-abortion lobbies at constituency level, 'It was inside Parliament that the battle was really won by the strategy, effort and organization of the pro-abortion lobby' (Marsh and Chambers 1981, p. 163). The failure of the Corrie Bill which sought to amend radically the 1967 Act 'shows how important a knowledge of parliamentary procedure is for parliamentary interest groups. The pro-abortion side was better versed in procedure, and on most occasions better at using it' (p. 191). Although both sides had very effective whipping systems to mobilise their supporters, the pro-abortion lobby was better organised (Marsh and Read 1988, p. 130).

Although the legalisation of abortion was influenced by evidence about the state of public opinion, having public opinion on your side is not sufficient to ensure the passage of a private member's bill. Polls conducted since 1958 have shown that a growing majority of the population favour the abolition of hunting, but in the decade between 1967 and 1977 sixteen anti-hunting bills failed to become law. This was partly because of the political skills of a group of pro-hunting Conservative MPs, and partly because of the 'vagaries of the procedures for Private Members' bills in the House of Commons' (Thomas 1983, p. 268). The League Against Cruel Sports decided that, rather than trying to pursue the fruitless route of private members' legislation, it would be better to use evidence of public opinion to persuade the Labour Party to adopt a manifesto commitment to abolish hunting. It was argued that 'only a government bill would succeed in passing all the parliamentary stages and only a manifesto commitment would be likely to get sufficient parliamentary time and attention to get the bill through the Lords' (p. 222). This decision represents a significant recognition of the limitations of private members' bills as a means for cause groups to attain their objectives.

## Pressure groups and the party system

In approaching ministers and MPs, pressure groups are dealing with members of political parties. Sometimes, party channels may be a useful means of bringing pressure to bear on a minister, as was noted in the discussion of the specialist backbench committees within the parliamentary parties. The focus in this section, however, is on influencing the political parties outside Parliament. As was noted in Chapter 1, there are some pressure groups that exist solely within political parties with the object of influencing their policies, but the discussion here will be concerned with pressure groups which use contacts with the political parties as a means of attaining their objectives.

There is a sense in which political parties and pressure groups are competitors: for members, for activists, and for influence. As political party membership has declined, pressure group membership has grown. There is, of course, not an 'either or' choice between the two. A person who is active in the Labour Party may, for example, also be involved in cause groups such as the Child Poverty Action Group and Shelter. However, there is probably some causal connection between the decline of party membership and the rise of a new generation of pressure groups. Individuals who have found the existing political parties too formal, hidebound and slow to attain results may have opted for the fresher and more innovative political policies and strategies being pursued by pressure groups. As Porritt and Winner (1988, p. 69) note, 'it is precisely the inability of the Labour Party to dig itself out of its own fossilized form of in-fighting which understandably makes Greens doubt that they are likely to embrace green politics at anything more than the most superficial level'.

It should also be noted that political parties may wish to use pressure groups as allies, particularly in the mobilisation of support. Thus, for example, when water privatisation legislation was introduced into Parliament in 1988, Labour's spokesperson on the issue announced her intention 'to enlist the help of outside pressure groups, such as Greenpeace and Friends of the Earth, to help press home the environmental protection case to the voters' (*Financial Times*, 7 December 1988). Similarly, in the 1970s the Conservatives set up a Private Enterprise Consultative Council, with eighteen trade associations as founder members, serviced by their Small Business Bureau. 'There is no doubt that it served the party's electoral interests to sympathize with, to encourage, small business organizations and to attempt to incorporate them' (Elliott *et al.* 1982, p. 83). Parties may also, however, be concerned with strengthening pressure groups to assist policy implementation. Worried about the lack of CBI influence over pay negotiations, a problem which would become more serious if an attempt were made to pursue a full employment policy, a group of social scientists close to the Labour Party discussed ways of improving the CBI's organisational strength in the run-up to the 1987 general election.

One of the main strategies used by pressure groups in relation to political parties is to seek to persuade them to adopt resolutions which will lead to a manifesto commitment to adopt the group's objectives. Such an approach is particularly relevant in relation to the Labour Party where the party conference has a greater formal role in making policy than in the Conservative Party. Thus, the anti-hunting lobby was able to get an appropriate resolution adopted by a constituency party. When this resolution was being processed through the Labour Party committee system:

> Discussion papers were prepared by Transport House staff who solicited information from the [League Against Cruel Sports] and other animal welfare organisations. The [British Field Sports Society] presented its views although these were submitted too late to have any effect on the early drafts of papers and in any case fell victim to the personal prejudices of the Transport House researcher.
>
> (Thomas 1983, p. 204)

The Conservative Party does not offer the same opportunities for exerting influence on a clearly defined and relatively democratic process for deciding party policy. However, lobbyists turn up in large numbers at the Conservative as well as at the Labour annual conference (and at the smaller party conferences as well), if only to keep in touch with the pulse of party opinion, and perhaps to seize the chance for a discreet word with a minister. When the Conservative Party had a Research Department concerned with policy development, this was often a more fruitful route for lobbying than the party conference or branch organisations. Field (1982, p. 61) notes that 'Relevant sections of Conservative party policy documents bear witness to the effectiveness of the [Child Poverty Action] Group's lobbying.' However, particularly in the Conservative Party in the 1980s, party bureaucracies are generally insufficiently permeable or influential on policy to be a useful major lobbying target.

Whiteley and Winyard (1987, p. 102) argue that 'party contacts are a relatively undeveloped aspect of the work of groups', in part because groups have absorbed a conventional wisdom which sees activists as party supporters rather than decision makers. In this connection, it is interesting that government relations divisions in large firms often give quite considerable attention to developments within the political parties, even monitoring the SNP. However, as one government relations manager stressed in an interview, 'We cannot be seen to be party political. One has to be delicate. The day that lobbying becomes a party political matter would be very bad for us.'

In general, however, links between pressure groups and political parties are not well developed. Except in special cases such as the anit-hunting lobby, developing overclose links with one political party would be counterproductive, as it would mean that the group would be influential only when that party was in power (and might not be very influential then because its support would be taken for granted). As pointed out in Chapter 1, pressure groups and political parties are essentially different political formations. Political parties wish to win office; in part to put a political programme into effect, but also to keep out the opposing party, and to give their leaders the opportunity of ministerial office. Pressure groups are not seeking office, and their objectives are highly specific rather than broadly based programmes; indeed, in many cases, they are seeking to ameliorate difficulties caused for their members as a result of the implementation of party programmes.

## Pressure groups and the media

The media play a crucial role in modern politics. As one former Cabinet minister has noted, 'The Cabinet increasingly, as the years go on, tends to be most concerned with the agenda that the press and media are setting out as the crucial issues before the nation at any time' (Boyle 1971, p. 109). It is therefore not surprising that the effective management of relations with the media has become a crucial skill for pressure groups.

The term 'media' covers a variety of forms of dissemination — television, radio, the press, etc. — and, within each of those forms, material that is targeted at a variety of audiences. Television thus carries mass audience programmes and also programmes likely to be watched by a very small audience interested in a particular issue. The press ranges from mass circulation tabloids, through 'quality' newspapers, to highly specialised journals and magazines.

Sometimes it will be advantageous for pressure groups to try and reach the largest possible audience through a medium such as the television news or a mass circulation newspaper. On other occasions, however, a more targeted approach may be desirable. It may be more appropriate to aim to influence 'informed opinion' through the 'quality' newspapers which are read by large numbers of decision makers. Current affairs radio programmes have a significant audience among politicians, even including the Prime Minister. Each 'policy community' will also tend to support its own specialist press. Kogan notes that by the 1970s there were as many as fifty educational journalists working for the educational press, or as educational correspondents for newspapers. However, Kogan argued that the educational press was being affected by the general decline of the educational service, and, in the view of some observers, was 'now becoming less important in affecting or reinforcing popular attitudes towards education' (Kogan 1975, p. 134).

Important interventions may come from unexpected sections of the media. Marsh and Chambers note that the Corrie abortion bill was attacked by the whole range of women's magazines. 'Most surprising was the strong attack on the Bill which came from *Woman's Own*, a magazine not known for its radical views and with a largely conservative readership' (Marsh and Chambers 1981, p. 133). Indeed, *Woman's Own* paid for an opinion poll which provided evidence of widespread public opposition to the Corrie bill which was sent by the magazine to all MPs just before the debate at report stage. One MP listed it as one of the reasons why the bill eventually failed (p. 146). More generally, 'The women's magazines carried the pro-abortion lobby's message far more widely than ever before, and not just to the more radical women. The anti-abortion groups lacked this kind of publicity' (p. 133).

One indication of the increased importance of the media is the greater attention it has been given in the 1970s and 1980s by established 'insider' groups, with many of them shifting from the 'low profile' to the 'high profile' insider category. Groups which in the past had relied largely on behind-the-scenes contacts in Whitehall found that such a strategy was no longer adequate; it was also necessary to try and create a favourable public image to reinforce their contacts with civil servants and politicians.

When setting out a future programme for the CBI, one of its leaders noted that 'the CBI must try more successfully to influence the general public and the electorate as a way of supporting the longer-term policy objectives which it will be promoting in the NEDC and directly with government' (Watkinson 1976, p. 148). In 1977 the CBI initiated an annual conference, a move which it described as the 'CBI "goes public" for the first time' (CBI Annual Report 1977, p 10). The increased importance of media coverage to the organisation is reflected in the listing in the 1977 annual report of the number of reporters attending the conference, the extent of radio and television coverage, and the number of column inches in the press about the conference. The Chemical Industries Association has commented that 'Efforts to redress the negative view of the chemical industry held by many sectors of the public continued to be one of the Association's major priorities' (Chemical Industries Association Activities Report 1986, p. 24).

It is not just sectional groups that have been giving a greater priority to media relations. Established cause groups have also revised their strategies to give a new emphasis to contacts with the press. For example, the Council for the Protection of Rural England (CPRE) was run for nearly forty years by a general secretary whose 'style of operation was through personal contact in the corridors of power. He fastidiously avoided embarrassing those whom he influenced or sought to influence' (Lowe and Goyder 1983, p. 75). The CPRE subsequently became more media conscious, with an increasingly sophisticated approach to the use of the media. Thus, when a new director was appointed in 1980, he 'had experience in advertising and freelance writing for television and radio' (p. 75).

Environmental groups have particularly benefited from media publicity because they are able to provide stories with a considerable visual impact, and a high human (or animal) interest content. Television has been particularly important to them; 'the tabloids have generally been a disaster area for environmental stories and are still happy to portray environmentalists as whingeing flat-earthers' (Porritt and Winner 1988, p. 98). Among the quality papers, however, even the more conservative have taken environmental issues seriously. Lowe and Goyder (1983, p. 76) explain:

> A major part of the attraction of environmental issues for the media is that they are public interest issues of a non-political (i.e. non-partisan) nature. Thus they provide an important outlet for campaigning and investigative journalism, even for newspapers that take a typically conservative stance on other matters, and for broadcasting services striving for a 'balanced' view.

## How pressure groups use the media

Contacts with the media are clearly important to a wide range of pressure groups. However, in what particular ways do pressure groups use the media? It is suggested that six distinct uses can be distinguished: visibility, information, climate, reactive response, influence and content.

*Visibility* refers to the use of the media to establish a presence, and to recruit and retain members. For example, a television programme called *The Animals Film* 'was an important moment in the growth of public awareness of animal exploitation' (Porritt and Winner 1988, p. 52). Letters to the press may identify individuals who are sympathetic to the pressure group's objectives and who could be useful recruits in its campaigning activities. Constant exposure for the group in the media reassures its membership that it is active, and helps in the retention of members. There is little point in recruiting a large number of new members as a result of a blitz of media activity if their interest cannot be engaged and their support retained.

The media can be an important source of *information* for pressure groups. 'Lobbyists scan the papers . . . in the search for stories, data, opinions and letters related to themselves' (Davies 1985, p. 181). Frank Field recalls how the Child Poverty Action Group carefully read the court page to produce a list of individuals who had access to the then prime minister (Field 1982, p. 54).

*Climate* refers to the long-term efforts of pressure groups to change the climate of opinion on an issue in a way that is favourable to their objectives. This may involve seeking to influence 'informed opinion' and decision makers, but it is also important to seek long-run changes in public values which set the context within which policy is made. 'Through their background campaigns, environmental groups in general have enhanced their public image and generated a climate of opinion sympathetic to environmental protection' (Lowe and Goyder 1983, p. 79).

*Reactive response* is necessary when a news story emerges that is relevant to a group's concerns or activities. Sometimes an organisation may have to react very quickly to an unfavourable story: for example, the egg industry was obliged to react in December 1988 to a statement by a junior minister, Edwina Currie, about allegedly extensive contamination of eggs by salmonella. In such circumstances, a group may be forced into a defensive stance. However, properly managed, such situations can be used to create favourable publicity, particularly for cause groups. The group may be invited on a television programme to explain its position, or can at least write to the press in response to editorials or letters from others.

Using the media as a means of exerting *influence* on government is clearly particularly important. Of course, ministers are not usually going to change their policies because of a newspaper editorial, although a campaign in the press may oblige them to make a response on a particular issue. Sometimes, the government can be embarrassed into changing its mind through leaks of its intentions. The classic case occurred in 1977 when the Child Poverty Action Group leaked Cabinet minutes indicating that the Government was intending to postpone introduction of the child benefit scheme. The decision was reversed, with trade union support mobilised by the leaks, and child benefit was phased in.

Media coverage can reinforce a case being made to civil servants by demonstrating that the matter is one of public concern. It may help to move the problem up the political agenda. Field recalls that one way of getting the CPAG's correspondence 'onto the top of the pile and read by ministers was to ensure publicity for the letters in the media ... ministers would then request an internal briefing, thereby getting the department's attention onto the issue being raised by the Group' (Field 1982, pp. 53–4). Lowe and Goyder show how environmental groups have been able to use media coverage to arouse public opinion and obtain a response from a previously indifferent government department. In relation to issues such as the introduction of lead-free petrol and against the introduction of heavier lorries, 'the intense media interest transformed what had previously been a humdrum administrative matter into a sensitive political issue' (Lowe and Goyder 1983, p. 79).

Publicity to exert influence requires a rather different strategy, however, from that used by a group seeking visibility to get established. At that stage, a variety of stunts may be a justifiable means of launching the group and attracting members. However, Whiteley and Winyard's research (1987, p. 130) makes it clear that groups can be damaged by irresponsible publicity. Civil servants do not like groups who appear to be more interested in television publicity than in serious negotiations. Explaining the difference between 'responsible' and 'irresponsible' publicity, Whiteley and Winyard (p. 120) comment:

> Responsible publicity meant coverage in the quality press about the group's activities and the needs of its clients. Primarily it involved a reasoned presentation of the group's case. It did not involve attacks on the character and motives of ministers and officials, or illegal demonstrations such as sit-ins in supplementary benefits offices. These were seen as counter-productive.

Finally, pressure groups may lobby the media directly and attempt to influence the *content* of its output. A meeting between environmentalists and Robert Maxwell led to a three-month campaign on environmental issues (Porritt and Winner 1988, p. 98). Various pressure groups have been concerned about scripts used on the radio series *The Archers*, which attracts seven million listeners. The programme's producers are 'heavily lobbied by all and sundry' (quoted in Porritt and Winner 1988, p. 127). When one of the younger characters caught the green bug and started investigating the use of bovine somatotrophin on dairy herds, complaints were received from the farming establishment.

Whiteley and Winyard (1987, p. 10) note that a number of changes in the political environment have produced a situation in which 'Ministers and officials who might have reacted with hostility to the publicity associated with lobbying activity in the 1980s now regard it as a more normal aspect of campaign strategy.' Certainly, media coverage is generally an asset for cause groups, whereas sectional groups are often obliged to give it a greater emphasis as a defensive response. However, it is also important to remember the limits of media publicity. It is essentially ephemeral in character (this is particularly true of television); the media's attention span on an issue is necessarily limited; and politicians may be able to stall on an issue until attention has shifted elsewhere. As Porritt and Winner (1987, p. 86) comment, 'If a nation's ecological wisdom were measured by the number of television programmes it makes about the environment, Britain would have little to worry about.' Media coverage is a means of changing the political agenda, but it is important not to underestimate the forces which produce continuity in political decision making.

## Pressure groups and the courts

Pressure groups make far less use of the courts in Britain than they do in the United States. There are a number of reasons why this is the case, but an important one is that the American legal system takes a more generous view of what constitutes 'legal standing' than is the case in Britain. 'In sum, US law erects the lowest entry barriers against both associations and individuals wishing to challenge administrative decisions in court' (Brickman *et al.* 1985, p. 110). Thus, public interest associations that would be restricted from taking legal action in Britain 'can sue with relative ease in the United States pursuant to specific statutes and judicially defined standing rules' (p. 126).

Legal actions are costly and can take a long time to complete. Even if a group wins a victory in litigation, government may reverse the decision in subsequent legislation. It is therefore not surprising that Whiteley and Winyard (1987, p. 108) found that the great majority of groups in their sample 'have not seen the judicial process as a significant focus of their activities in attempting to influence policy making'. Test cases were mainly seen as a means of influencing the implementation stage of the policy process. They can sometimes be useful as 'an opportunity to politicize an issue and to exert pressure for changes in the law' (p. 108).

There may be cases where pressure groups resort to the courts when other strategies have failed. Following the defeat of the Corrie bill, the anti-abortion lobby switched its attention away from attempts to amend the 1967 Act in Parliament. As one alternative, they used the courts 'to attempt to establish a body of case law which would ensure that doctors were more circumspect and therefore less liberal in their interpretation of the Abortion Act' (Marsh and Read 1988, p. 132).

Court action has been used quite extensively by groups belonging to the 'moral right', concerned about what they see as the decline of traditional moral standards, or the excesses of the trade unions. Mary Whitehouse's National Viewers' and Listeners' Association has, for example, brought a number of court actions, particularly against the broadcasting authorities. The National Association for Freedom (NAFF) has also made extensive use of court actions, although expensive and dramatic cases were replaced by a 'whole series of modest legal battles up and down the country, mainly cases where NAFF is involved in supporting workers dismissed because they refuse to join a closed shop' (Elliott *et al.* 1982, p. 81). For groups such as NAFF the law seems to be used 'as a means of registering and publicizing its indignation' (p. 81). In general, the courts seem to be used by groups who cannot attain their objectives by more conventional methods.

## Local government

The 1980s have seen a significant reduction in the independence and powers of local government in Britain through a variety of changes ranging from the 'rate capping' of some authorities to the abolition of others. Nevertheless, local authorities still take many significant decisions in areas such as education and planning, and therefore become the focus of pressure group activity. Occasionally, the actions of a local authority may attract the attention of a national pressure group such as the CBI. More generally, however, the pressure group is purely local in character. A considerable number of organisations exist at the local level: Newton (1976) identified 4,264 in his study of Birmingham. Many of these organisations are not primarily political in character. For example, they may be engaged in a variety of leisure activities ranging from swimming to ballroom dancing. However, such groups may become actively involved in local politics if their activities are threatened in some way — if, for example, an allotment society or a football club is told that its council-owned site is to be developed for housing.

In such cases, existing organisations with memberships and funds can be mobilised to lobby councillors, and officers become drawn into the local political process. In many other cases, a loose campaigning group is formed to fight on a particular issue such as a projected school closure, a new road, or a new development. Once the issue is resolved one way or the other, the group dissolves. Relatively informal groupings of this kind are emerging and disappearing all the time at the local level; in one sense, they could be regarded as a healthy flowering of local democracy, although they often lack the resources and inside knowledge available to the decision makers. Moreover, such groups are often seeking to protect rather narrow interests, so that 'sporadic interventionism' assumes a 'highly individual and unorganised form with affected people arguing against one another for personal compensation and benefit' (Dowse and Hughes 1977, p. 90).

There are, however, some more permanent 'primary' pressure groups at the local level. One important category is the local amenity society, which may be a branch of the CPRE or may have a purely local title such as 'The Henley Society' or 'The Leamington Society'. By 1975 there were about 1,200 such societies throughout the country (Lowe and Goyder 1983, p. 89). For a variety of reasons, including the technical knowledge possessed by their members, their 'responsible' stance, and their appeal to broadly based values rather than narrow interests, such organisations tend to have a close working relationship with their local authorities. For example, 'It is common practice for local amenity societies to be consulted regularly on planning applications' (p. 97).

Another very important category of local pressure group is the chamber of commerce or chamber of trade, representing local business interests. (Chambers of trade have traditionally been organisations of local retailers, with perhaps some membership from other small business interests, while chambers of commerce have a much broader membership including large businesses in the locality.) The larger chambers of commerce have considerable resources and substantial staffs (for example, well over a hundred in Brimingham). At the other end of the spectrum is 'the tattered, decrepit and inefficient image offered by the smaller Chambers' (Stewart 1984, p. 44). One chamber, appealing for donations of such equipment as a teapot, cups and saucers, noted that 'the first floor over a small newsagent's shop is not the best of locations for the Commercial Centre of the Borough's Business Activity' (quoted in Stewart 1984, p. 44).

However, it is clear that some of the more effective chambers have developed a close, 'insider group' relationship with their local authorities. For example, a study of the Norwich chamber found that all major planning applications were shown to the chamber, and city and chamber officials made a joint site visit where commercial sites were involved (Grant 1983). Chambers have also become closely involved in the implementation of inner city policy, as 'local authorities are obliged by the [Department of the Environment] to consult Chambers and Commerce before schemes to be included in the urban programme can go forward to central government' (King 1985, p. 207). Under the Thatcher Government, chambers of commerce have tended to acquire new responsibilities in relation to local authorities, being seen as the authentic voice of the small entrepreneur and as a means of restraining any excesses by local government.

In rural areas, farmers and landowners are an important interest, often, of course, directly represented in significant numbers on local authorities. A study of Suffolk found that there was a close, harmonious and informal relationship between the National Farmers' Union and the Country Landowners' Association on the one hand, and the planning authorities on the other. It was observed that:

> the agricultural interest and the 'public interest' are synonymous, or are at least seen to be so. Indeed, the identification drawn by local and country planners between the two has resulted in a marked reluctance on the part of local authorities to invoke such powers as they may have in order to force farmers to observe regulations which may hinder the profitability of agricultural enterprises.
>
> (Newby et al. 1978, p. 235)

Some areas have trade councils which bring together trade unions in the locality, but they have tended to diminish in significance over time. In practice, the local government unions such as NALGO are an important force in defending the interests of their members, which can include opposing major changes in local authority policy that involve cutbacks in services – as happened, for example, when the Conservatives won control of Bradford city council in 1988.

The voluntary sector (for example, Councils for Voluntary Service, Age Concern) is of increasing importance at the local level, particularly as it is often responsible for the delivery of services funded by the local authority. Stoker (1988, p. 124) argues that 'given the rise of self-help organisations within the sector and a more general willingness to engage in campaigning activity, the potential for and likely effectiveness of voluntary sector lobbying of local authorities has also been considerably enhanced'.

In some areas there are local ratepayers' associations, although they are not as active or as prominent as they were when major rates increases were experienced in the mid-1970s. Many of these associations, particularly those that emerged in the 1970s, were classic 'outsider' groups, making general accusations of bureaucratic empire-building and extravagance, but offering 'remarkably little in the way of constructive suggestions as to how the [rates] increases might be kept down' (Nugent 1979, p. 33). Indeed, many ratepayers' movements have become so frustrated at their inability to influence council policy that they have crossed the divide between pressure group and party activity and formed purely local parties to contest council elections (see Grant 1978).

## Insider and outsider groups in local politics

In many ways, the distinction between 'insider' and 'outsider' groups has often seemed to be more marked at the local than the national level. Policy is largely formed through 'discussions between officers and councillors, but some groups may be granted an established consultative relationship, if only as a means of explaining the local authority's policy to interested audiences. 'Many planning authorities now regard a close collaborative relationship with responsible environmental groups as an important political resource in establishing good relations for official planning as well as in delivering public consent for particular policies and decisions' (Lowe and Goyder 1983, p. 95). Moreover, there has been a more general 'opening out' by at least some authorities, which provides new opportunities for interest group activity and influence (see Stoker 1988, pp. 120–4).

What is clear is that there is considerable variation from one local authority area to another, both in terms of the patterns of interest group activity and the receptiveness of local councils to their representations. Stoker suggests that the difference between localities may be captured in terms of a fourfold categorisation. Left-wing Labour authorities in urban areas try to develop good relations with cause and community groups, including those representing women and ethnic minorities. Good relations with trade unions may contrast with antagonistic relationships with business groups. In urban areas with centre-right Labour (or centre party influenced) authorities, there is an apparent commitment to good relations with a range of groups, but this may be offset by a suspicion of some organisations which are seen as acting as a front for extremists or Conservatives. In suburban and rural locations, Conservative or centre party influenced councils may be well disposed to the formal end of the voluntary sector and to the environmental and amenity lobby, but some interests (such as those of agricultural workers or persons on the housing waiting list) may be disregarded. In areas where 'New Right' Conservatives are in office 'there is likely to be a willingness to work closely with a select group of middle-class residents' associations, amenity groups and business interests. However, these local authorities are actively hostile to any groups they consider left-wing' (p. 126).

Such an approach, which emphasises the politics of the controlling party as the key variable, provides an alternative to conceptualisations of local authority decision making in terms of a technocratic model that emphasises the power that officers derive from their professional expertise, or the sharing of power by a joint élite of senior councillors and officers (see Wilson 1988). Whichever model one adopts, however, the extent to which pressure groups are able to exert influence is significantly affected by the attitudes towards them of councillors and/or local authority officers.

In general, there is not the same tradition of long-term, routine consultation as at the national level. This is accentuated by the fact that local pressure groups generally have fewer resources in terms of their own staff than their national counterparts, whilst local authority officers are less dependent on them as a source of information and consent than civil servants.

Consider, for example, the closure of a small school in a rural area, an event which often arouses considerable controversy in the affected locality. County council officials will have all the information they need about central government policy on such matters, on the costs of the particular school, and on the likely future demand for places there. They will have no difficulty in presenting a policy paper without consulting outside groups. An organisation formed to fight the closure may be able to accumulate expertise on the issue, particularly if it has some well-educated and well-informed members, but they will not be able to compete with the expertise possessed by the full-time officials of the county council. They may be able to win the support of their local councillor, but this may have little effect in an authority tightly controlled by the ruling party.

Although citizen groups fighting local authority policies often have an uphill battle, there is scope for pressure group activity at the local level. As a number of the examples discussed suggest, the range and effectiveness of such activity would appear to be growing.

# 5

# Pressure Groups and the European Community

The approach of the projected completion of the European internal market in 1992 has renewed interest in the political processes of the European Community. However, apart from some monographs (Kirchner and Swaiger 1981; Butt Philip 1985) and some more detailed studies of particular areas of activity (for example, Sargent 1987), pressure groups and the European Community has been a relatively neglected subject. In part, this may reflect a disappointment that pressure groups have not played the positive role in the process of unification assigned to them by integration theorists. It also reflects the fact that the impact of the Community has varied from one policy area to another, with some causes (such as abortion or hunting) not being a matter for the Community. Even within the areas covered by the treaties, the impact of Community initiatives has been uneven.

In addition there is also a more general conceptual difficulty for British analysts in coping with a new political situation of which they have no experience, one in which political authority is shared with institutions beyond the boundaries of the nation state. Indeed, there are no real precedents for the attempt to bind together a group of diverse nation states with different histories, economies, cultures, languages and political institutions. It is therefore not surprising that the Community has often been conceptualised as something external to the British political system, rather than an integral and increasingly important part of it.

Perhaps the best way to think of the Community is as a confederation of states in which some matters are largely the responsibility of the Community authorities, others are shared, and yet others are likely to remain largely the prerogative of the national government. The precise way in which this confederative arrangement will develop, even after 1992, remains uncertain. National 'political loyalties, and a desire to maintain national sovereignty in such areas as taxation policy, remain strong. However, the Community already has some statelike characteristics, in terms of its ability to make authoritative decisions. The influence of the Community over agricultural policy is well known; perhaps less appreciated is the fact that it is largely responsible for trade policy, and is increasingly influential in areas such as environmental policy, competition policy and transport policy.

The complexity of the Community's own decision-making processes, and of the relationships between the member states and the Community, has perhaps dissuaded some analysts from probing too deeply into this area. One general point that should be appreciated is that, apart from exceptions in, for example, certain areas of agricultural policy, the Community is largely dependent on the co-operation of the member states for the implementation of its policies. This means that policies are often implemented with considerable delay, half-heartedly or inefficiently, or even not at all (although open neglect or defiance will ultimately lead to a member state being brought before the European Court of Justice). Indeed, Scharpf (1988) argues that the European Community suffers from a 'joint decision trap' which produces suboptimal decisions. This is a consequence of a situation in which Community decisions are directly dependent upon the agreement of member states under conditions of near unanimity.

Scharpf convincingly argues that the European Community is organised around a series of 'policy communities' similar to those found at the national level:

> At the institutional level, the Community is unequivocally supported by the self-interest of the vertical alliances of policy specialists − interest associations, national ministries and parliamentary committees, and the large contingents of specialized lobbyists, bureaucrats and politicians operating at the European level.
>
> (Scharpf 1988, p. 270)

The vertical segmentation of these 'policy communities' is, however, complicated by the way in which domestic political forces become transmitted to the European level. For example, environmental groups (notably the Green Party) are particularly strong in West Germany.

Environmentally sensitive industries in West Germany such as chemicals do not wish to be the subject of more stringent regulations than in other EC countries. Hence, it is in their interest for such issues to be resolved at the European level. They may be able to mobilise support from other member states to modify the demands being made and, at worst, they can ensure that the same regulations have to be observed by competitor firms in other EC countries. In this way, political pressures originating in West Germany transmit themselves through the political machinery of the EC so that they affect environmental regulation in Britain.

The annual reports of most industry trade associations in Britain show an increasing emphasis on EC affairs. Table 5.1 provides information on the EC activities and European association memberships of a selection of specialised food and drink industry associations. Many of the matters being dealt with are highly technical, but they are nevertheless of crucial importance to the industry concerned. For many business associations, EC activities are becoming the most important part of their work. For example, the 1987 annual report of the Food and Drink Federation (FDF) comments, 'The FDF's activity during 1987 increasingly took place within the context of the European Community and the growing amount of legislation emanating from Brussels.' The Chemical Industries Association (CIA) noted in its 1984 Activities Report, 'We are increasingly working in an environment where directives and regulations designed and enacted in the Community have a profound influence on the daily life of our industry, our member companies, and all their employees in one way or another.'

The European Community is thus an important arena for pressure group activity. It is also a fertile ground for such activity, in the sense that the Community adopts a generally 'welcoming' approach to pressure groups, particularly if they are organised on a Europe-wide basis. This extends particularly to the persistence of corporatist notions, with an emphasis on the special importance of the 'social partners' (employers, unions, etc.) that does not go down well with the Thatcher Government, particularly when it is linked to the idea of a 'Social Europe'.

Pressure groups have three main avenues of approach in seeking to influence the EC:

1. Working at the national level to influence the stance taken by their national government in EC discussions, and to influence the implementation of EC decisions.
2. Working through European-level federations of national pressure

**Table 5.1** European activities of selected food and drink industry associations in 1987

|  | European level association | Activities related to EC |
|---|---|---|
| British Essence Manufacturers Association | European Flavour Industry Assoc. | Representations to MAFF and EC Commission on draft EC Framework Directive on Flavourings |
| British Fruit and Vegetable Canners Association | OEITFL | Revisions to EC Labelling Directive; discussions in OEITFL on the setting of standard drained weights for canned fruit and vegetables to avoid the application of unit pricing |
| British Maize Refiners Association | AAM | Revision of the EC starch regime; discussions with MAFF on methods to calculate starch purity for production refunds; EC proposals for the harmonisation of the Customs Tariff System |
| Fish and Meat Spreadable Products Association | CLITRAVI | EC proposal to discontinue exemption from datemarking for products with a shelf life of over eighteen months; proposals for an EC Directive on Fish Hygiene |
| Infant and Dietetic Foods Association | IDACE | Proposal for an EC Directive on Infant Formulae and Follow-up Milks (governing compositional standards, advertising and marketing); EC Framework Directive on Foodstuffs for Particular Nutritional Uses |
| UK Preserves Manufacturers Association | OEITFL | Application of monetary compensation amounts on preserves as part of annual farm price negotiations; EC proposal to amend the Preserves Directive, representations made to the Commission through OEITFL |

groups (the 1980s have seen the emergence of some direct membership associations at the European level, a particularly significant development in terms of the creation of a European political identity).

3. Making direct representations in Brussels; this is a less common channel than the other two, but can be very important on occasions.

The analysis in this chapter will be structured around a consideration of these three distinct channels of access, as well as considering some illustrative case studies. For those readers not familiar with the various Community institutions, a brief review of them is provided in Figure 5.1. It must be stressed that this is a very simplified account, and cannot substitute for the reading of book-length studies of EC decision making.

## Influencing the Community through the national government

Divergent national interests remain a significant feature of Community politics. A pressure group whose views on a particular issue diverge from those of its European counterparts may decide that the best course of action is to persuade the British government to argue its point of view within the Council of Ministers. Equally, such a strategy can be used to reinforce representations being made in Brussels when associated pressure groups in different EC countries agree on the approach to be adopted. It must be emphasised that operating through the national government is often used in conjunction with alternative means of exerting pressure.

Such a method of approach enables groups to make use of their existing contacts at the national level. It is therefore often not too difficult to win the British government round to their point of view, particularly if attention can be drawn to a distinctive British national interest. If the British government then adheres to its position in the Council of Ministers, it will be difficult, even under a system of qualified majority

---

1. The *European Council* consists of meetings of the heads of government held at six-monthly intervals. It originated in summits held between 1969 and 1974, formalised into a European Council by a decision of the December 1974 Paris summit. Preparatory negotiations for such meetings may be as important as the meetings themselves. Scharpf (1988, p. 268) notes that 'the establishment of the European Council should be seen as a symbol of the increasing importance of European policy choices and as an attempt to assert the control of national policy generalists over the vertical alliances of policy specialists dominating the Council of Ministers as well as the European Commission'.

2. The *Council of Ministers* is the real legislative body of the European Community. It is made up of the responsible ministers from each member state. Thus, as well as the original 'general' Council of (Foreign) Ministers, it can and does meet as a Council of Agriculture

Ministers, a Council of Transport Ministers, a Council of Energy Ministers, etc. Since the ratification of the Single European Act in 1987, decisions no longer have to be unanimous. However, unanimity is preserved for some matters such as border controls, and 54 votes out of 76 are needed for a qualified majority, a high threshold. Hence, decisions emerge through a complicated and lengthy process of bargaining.

3. This process of bargaining is facilitated by the *Committee of Permanent Representatives* (COREPER). Each member state has an ambassador in Brussels and these meet together in COREPER, their work being supported by groups of experts dealing with particular issues. COREPER prepares the ground for Council of Ministers meetings by narrowing down the areas of disagreement.

4. The *Commission* is often used as a general term to refer to the EC bureaucracy headquartered in the Berlaymont building in Brussels. More strictly, it is the various commissioners (each with a particular portfolio) meeting as a collectivity (the larger states nominate two commissioners; the smaller states one). The civil servants servicing the Commission are organised in a series of twenty directorate-generals or departments covering, for example, agriculture, the environment and energy. The Commission has a crucial role in the preparation of legislation for consideration by the Council of Ministers. 'The main centres of power within the Community remain the Council of Ministers and the Commission ... the Commission proposes, while the Council disposes' (Butt Philip 1985, p.18).

5. The *European Parliament* is a directly elected body. Its powers have grown over the years, particularly in the area of the budget, but are ultimately circumscribed by the fact that real legislative authority resides in the Council of Ministers representing the member states. The Parliament's real work is done by its specialist committees which, significantly, meet in Brussels rather than Strasbourg.

6. The *Economic and Social Committee* was specifically established to represent economic and social interest groups in the EC. It offers comments on Commission proposals. It is not generally regarded as a crucial forum by pressure groups.

7. The *European Court of Justice* interprets the Community treaties and the legislation flowing from them. It resolves disputes between the Community and the member states, obliging them to enforce Community decisions where they have failed to do so. 'The Community's use of its own system of law to enforce its decisions marks it off from almost every other international organisation and is one of the foremost reasons for its effectiveness' (Butt Philip 1985, p. 66).

**Figure 5.1**  European Community Institutions

voting, to make it give way. This is particularly the case when the issue has attracted support at a high political level. There is always a risk, however, that the government will bargain away its stance as part of one of the complex deals that are often the only way of breaking the logjam of Community decision making. As Butt Philip (1985, p. 57) notes, 'The national pressure groups will be very much in the hands of government officials once the Council of Ministers' negotiations begin.'

The extent to which national channels of representation are used will vary from group to group and from issue to issue, and even within the lifetime of a particular issue. All the available options will be combined in whatever seems to be the mix likely to secure the desired outcome. However, a review of the EC activities of business associations led to the conclusion that the groups studied:

> clearly attached high priority to channels which could be operationalised at national level . . . Channels of representation to the Commission through British Government officials were preferred whenever possible to direct channels of representation to the Commission.
>
> (Sargent 1987, pp. 228–9)

The way in which national channels of access may be used in combination with other methods of exerting influence can be illustrated by the FDF's campaign on the Commission's proposed tax on vegetable and marine oils and fats (in effect, a tax on margarine). The FDF won Government support for its opposition to this proposal by pointing out that it would have serious inflationary consequences, increasing the UK's food bill by £300 million per year. It would also undermine Government health policies by penalising unsaturated vegetable oils and fats. MAFF formed an Oils and Fats Tax Liaison Group, involving a number of trade associations. 'The purpose of this group was to marshal arguments and action against an oil and fats tax' (FDF Annual Report 1986, p. 15). The FDF recognised in its 1987 annual report that it has 'enjoyed the invaluable support of the UK Government' and that 'The Prime Minister's unflinching resistance to the tax has so far prevented adoption of the Commission's proposal.'

However, the FDF did not make the mistake of relying simply on the UK's ability to block the proposal at Community level. It also campaigned within the EC, lobbying MEPs and 'sister associations' in other member countries. Another tactic used was to seek support in third countries. For example, it drew attention to the damage the proposal would inflict on the economies of Third World countries supplying oilseeds. It also used the argument that the proposal ran counter to the principles of the General Agreement on Tariffs and Trade and might provoke a trade war between the EC and the USA.

The implementation of policy also provides opportunities for pressure groups to use their contacts with British civil servants. The detailed implementation of the Common Agricultural Policy (for example, the fixing of levies and export restitutions on particular commodities) is the responsibility of Management Committees. There is one of these committees, made up of representatives from each member state, for each of the commodities for which the EC has a market regime. It is clearly important for pressure groups interested in the work of these Management Committees to keep in touch with the national officials serving on them.

Most implementation of Community decisions is, however, the responsibility of national governments. Occasionally, a government may refuse to implement a Community decision until required to do so by the Court of Justice, as happened with the tachograph regulation in the late 1970s. Faced with opposition from the Transport and General Workers' Union, the Labour Government failed to implement the regulation until the Court ruled. 'Once the Court had delivered its adverse judgement in 1978 the British government was able to say to those interest groups opposed to the tachograph that it had no option but to enforce the EEC regulation' (Butt Philip 1985, p. 73).

A more usual pattern is detailed negotiations between pressure groups and civil servants about the implementation of an EC regulation. The pressure group should, of course, have at the negotiations stage identified implementation problems which would affect its members in a significant way and drawn the attention of civil servants to any anticipated difficulties. Very often, therefore, a pressure group will be satisfied with the regulations introduced by the British government. Thus, for example, the British Soluble Coffee Manufacturers Association welcomed the Coffee and Coffee Products (Amendment) Regulations which came into effect on 2 December 1987, implementing the EC Council Soluble Coffee Directive 85/573/EC. In other cases, long drawn-out negotiations may be necessary. For example, the Chemical Industries Association was closely involved in discussions on the drafting of Health and Safety Commission regulations on the control of substances hazardous to health designed to simplify the implementation of 'daughter' directives to the Framework Directive on Chemical, Physical and Biological Agents at Work. In particular, the CIA complained about 'the unnecessary complexity and over-ambitious nature of the proposals in the first consultative document' (CIA Activities Report 1985, p. 21).

## European-level pressure groups

Although pressure groups use their customary contacts at the national level to influence the development of EC legislation, they also employ the European-level federations of national pressure groups in a variety of ways. A national association may be able to press its case effectively on a particular issue through the European-level federation. For example, the Spice Trade Association, working via the European Spice Association, was successful in 1987 in excluding herbs and spices from the scope of the proposed amendments to the Unit Pricing Directive. In other instances, a European-level pressure group may be used to influence the government of another country. Thus, in 1987 EUVEPRO, the European association for the vegetable protein industry, persuaded the EC Commission to take up the question of West Germany's restrictive meat-product purity laws with the German Government and the Eruopean Court of Justice. ACFASOLE, the European soluble coffee mnaufacturers' association, has been concerned with the issue of subsidies received by Brazilian manufacturers.

Sargent's study of business associations suggests, however, that European-level associations are often used as a means of influencing counterpart associations in other member countries:

> The value of European interest groups as channels of representation to the groups' sister federations was twofold. First, to establish the degree of support they could expect from their counterparts in other EC member states for their views on EC related matters, specifically those of vital interest to British groups. Secondly, to encourage their sister federations to support their British counterparts' views, not only through collective representations but also through their own individual representations to EC bodies and to their respective national governments.
>
> (Sargent 1987, p. 232)

There are a considerable number of pressure groups operating at the EC level. A list of formally recognised groups issued by the Commission in 1980 included 439 groups, of which 40 per cent were industrial trade associations; a third were connected with agriculture and food; and the remainder were a variety of commercial, service industry, trade union, consumer and environmental interests (figures from Butt Philip 1985, pp. 27–9). As Butt Philip recognises, these figures are an understatement of the total number of groups.

Table 5.2 lists associations operating at the EC level in just one industry, chemicals (excluding pharmaceuticals). Nine major sectoral or subsectoral associations and sixty-five product-level associations are identified (the list is almost certainly incomplete). New organisations are being formed all the time. For example, the European BHT Manufacturers Association was formed in 1987 to monitor and co-ordinate safety, toxicity and regulatory aspects of butylated hydroxytoluene (BHT is used as an antioxidant in food, plastics and other products). On the whole, it is the larger producer groups that are best organised in terms of resources (see Table 5.3), although many of the smaller associations dealing with a particular product are run by one executive and a secretary, or are run from the offices of a sectoral association.

What is the motivation for the formation of European-level associations dealing with particular products or processes? They are often dealing with highly technical issues which are nevertheless very important to their member firms, and often to society more generally. Taking two examples from Table 5.2, the Automobile Emissions Control by Catalysts Group was formed in 1985 by the European producers of catalysts and substrates for catalytic converters. They were keen to see the catalytic converter introduced in European cars through the introduction of legislation similar to that in the USA. They are a publicity-oriented group, staging an exhibition in the Houses of Parliament, and inviting British journalists and parliamentarians to test the performance of cars fitted with catalytic converters. They have also been accepted as observers in the Motor Vehicle Emissions Group of DG III of the Commission.

The technical bureau for inorganic feed phosphates has been concerned with the correct customs classification of some of the products imported into the EC, and an EC draft directive on feeding stuffs which, it is argued, would allow some manufacturers to use low-quality products, creating a source of unfair competition. It has also been concerned with an EC Directive limiting the amount of cadmium in feed phosphates, which was passed very quickly. This could have a major impact on the industry as cadmium-poor raw materials are limited, and there is at present no economically viable process which can be used to remove the cadmium. This offers a good example of a way in which a product association with an apparently technical focus may be concerned with a matter of vital importance to an industry's future.

**Table 5.2** European-level associations representing the chemical industry (excluding pharmaceuticals)

---

*Major sector and subsector associations*

CEFIC (Conseil Européen des Fédérations de l'Industrie Chimique)

Association of Petrochemicals Producers in Europe (APPE)

Association of Plastics Manufacturers in Europe (APME)

Association Internationale de la Savonnerie et de la Détergence (AIS)

Comité Européen des Associations de Fabricants de Peintures, d'Encres d'Imprimerie et de Couleurs d'Art (CEPE)

Comité Marché Commun de l'Industrie des Engrais Azotés et Phosphates (CMC)

Comité de Liaison des Associations Européennes de l'Industrie de la Parfumerie, des Produits Cosmetiques et de Toilette (COLIPA)

Committee of Plastics Converters' Associations of Western Europe (EUTRAPLAST)

Groupement International des Associations Nationales de Fabricants de Produits Agrochimiques (GIFAP) (global organisation)

*Product-level associations*

Acetone Sector Group

Acrylonitrile Sector Group

Activated Carbons Producers Association

Aluminium Sulphate Producers Association

Aminoplast Glues Sector Group

Aromatics Sector Group

Association Européenne des Producteurs d'Acides Gras (APAG)

Association for the Study of Safety Problems in the Production and Use of Propellant Powders (EASSP)

Association of European Manufacturers of Sporting Ammunition (AFEMS)

Automobile Emissions Control by Catalysts (AECC)

Bromine Sector Group

Bureau International Technique de l'"ABS'

Bureau International Technique de l'Anhydride Phthalique (PA)

Bureau International Technique du Chlore (BITC)

Bureau International Technique des Solvants Chlorés (BITSC)

Bureau International Technique des 'Inorganic Feed Phosphates'

Bureau International Technique des Gélatines

Bureau International Technique des Plastifiants

Bureau International Technique des Polysters insaturés

Bureau International Technique du Spathfluor

Cadmium Pigment Producers Association (CPA)

Centre Européen d'Etudes de l'Acide Sulfurique (CEFAS)

Centre Européen des Silicones (CES)

Centre International d'Etudes du Lindane

Choline Chloride Producers Association

Ecological and Toxicological Association of the Dyestuffs Manufacturing Industry (ETAD) (global organisation)

Ethylene Oxide and Derivatives Sector Group

European Association of Fatty Acid Producing Companies (APAG)

European Butylated Hydroxytoluene Manufacturers Association (EBMA)

European Catalysts Manufacturers Association (ECMA)

European Center of Studies on Linear Alkylbenzene (LAB ECOSOL)

European Chemical Industry Ecology and Toxicology Centre (ECETOC)
European Citric Acid Manufacturers Association (ECAMA)
European Council of Vinyl Manufacturers (ECVM)
European Fluorocarbon Technical Committee (EFCTC)
European Food Emulsifier Manufacturers Association (EFEMA)
European Food Phosphates Producers Association (EFPA)
European Fuel Oxygenates Association (EFOA)
European Isopropanol Producers Association (EIPPA)
European Lead Stabilizers Association (ELSA)
European Methylbromide Association (EMA)
European Nitrators Association (ENA)
European Photochemical Industry (EPI)
European Plastic Film, Membrane and Covering Manufacturers' Association
    (AEC)
European Producers Association of Detergent Alkylates
European Technical Committee for Fluorine (CTEF)
European Wax Federation (EWF)
Federation of European Explosive Manufacturers (FEEM)
Fluorocarbon Technical Committee (EFCTC)
Methanol Sector Group
Methylamines Producers Association
Methylene Chloride Sector Group
Methyl Ethyl Ketone Sector Group
Methylmethacrylate Sector Group (MNA)
Oxygenated Solvents Sector Group
Peroxygen Sector Group
Phenol Sector Group
Phthalic Anhydride Sector Group
Plasticizer Range Alcohols Sector Group
Polymethylmethacrylate Producers Association (PMMA)
Product Committee Surfactants (CESIO)
Sodium Cyanide Sector Group
Styrene Producers Association
Titanium Dioxide Manufacturers Sector Group (SGTM)
Zinc Oxide Producers Association (ZOPA)

## The problem of different national interests

The effectiveness of European-level associations is limited not so much
by the organisational resources available to them as by the difficulty of
reconciling the different national interests of the member associations.
For example, at the first meeting of the food industry organisation, CIAA,
as an independent body, the British chairman felt compelled to call for
'a readiness on the part of each delegation to concede a little here and
there and not to stay adamant in the defence to the last syllable of a
position obviously unacceptable to the Committee as a whole' (*FDIC
Bulletin*, no. 21, p. 7). Because of the difficulty of reconciling national

**Table 5.3** Principal European interest groups: date founded, staff size and budget (ranked by staff size)

|  | Date established | Total number of full- and part-time staff | Approximate budget 1988 (£) |
|---|---|---|---|
| Committee of Agricultural Organisations in the EC (COPA) | 1958 | 44 | 1.5m |
| European Council of Chemical Manufacturers' Federations (CEFIC) | 1972[1] | 42 | N/A |
| Union of Industries in the European Community (UNICE) | 1958 | 29 | 1.3m |
| European Trade Union Confederation (ETUC) | 1973 | 28 | N/A |
| European Bureau of Consumers Unions (BEUC) | 1962 | 10 | 300,000 |
| Committee of Family Organisations in the EC (COFACE) | 1979 | 8 | 180,000 |
| European Environmental Bureau (EEB) | 1974 | 7 | 130,000 |
| Association of Plastics Manufacturers in Europe (APME) | 1975 | 6 | N/A |
| Confederation of the Food and Drink Industries of the EC (CIAA) | 1981 | 6 | 375,000 |
| European Community of Consumer Co-operatives (EUROCOOP) | 1957 | 5 | N/A |

[1]Merged from two predecessor organisations.
*Sources*: Own data; *Consumers and the Common Agricultural Policy* (London: HMSO, 1988, reproduced by permission of the Controller).

differences of opinion, European-level organisations often produce 'lowest common denominator' policies which are so generally worded that their impact on the development of Community policy is minimal.

With the impending completion of the internal market, this pattern of ineffectual representation cannot be tolerated for ever. One response has, of course, been for national groups to make their own representations direct to the Commission (this channel of access is discussed further below). However, such contacts do not compensate for the failure of many sectors of industry to develop a coherent European policy to match the Europe-wide policies being developed and implemented by the Community. The most effective steps in the direction of developing a new pattern of representation have been taken by the chemical industry, which is particularly affected by Community policy.

### Effective organisation in the chemical industry

In the European Council of Chemical Manfacturers' Federations (CEFIC) the industry already had a relatively effective European-level association of associations. With a staff of over forty, and about 1,500 representatives from national associations and companies on committees, CEFIC is a well-resourced association. However, there was concern within the industry that the hundred person-years of senior executive time that was being put into CEFIC each year was not achieving commensurate results. It was felt that the way forward was to achieve a Europe-wide chemical industry consensus at the highest level, that is, at the level of the senior executives of the major chemical companies. In order to achieve this objective, changes had to be made in CEFIC's structure to achieve more direct participation in decision making by companies as distinct from national association staff.

The first reform introduced under Sir John Harvey-Jones's presidency was the introduction of a new category of corporate associate member, open, in effect, to major multinationals. Through an annual assembly, these major companies elect members to the Committee of Directors, which discusses major issues and provides the mandate of the committees and working parties that discuss issues in detail. These changes were seen not as a bureaucratic detail, but as a key theme for the British presidency, building 'new bridges between the Federations who are the legal members of CEFIC and the major trans-national companies operating in several member states whose practical and financial support and commitment is essential to the success of CEFIC in all its European and international lobbying activities' (CIA Activities Report 1986, p. 14).

The second major reform was the formation of an Association of Petrochemicals Producers in Europe (APPE) to replace a number of uncoordinated CEFIC and non-CEFIC committee and *ad hoc* groups. However, this is not simply an organisational tidying up. The significance of APPE is that it is a direct membership association of major multinational companies operating at the European level. The future development of effective industry representation at the European level is likely to rely increasingly on such organisations. Another significant development in this general area is the adoption of joint positions by top-level European industrialists, circumventing the slow decision-making procedures of associations of associations, such as the Round Table of European industrialists and the Group of 12 concerned with information technology. The Round Table is made up of forty heads of major

European industrial companies and is chaired by the head of the supervisory board of Philips, the Dutch electronics giant.

## The limitations of the internal political market

The completion of the internal market should, ideally, be complemented by changes in the internal political market. One British association director suggested in interview that his industry would ultimately be represented by one Europe-wide association, with subnational branches in the member states. However, the experience of confederations like that of Canada suggests that such organisations take a long time to emerge, and that loose groupings are a common pattern at the confederal level. Certainly, in the European Community, national associations are not generally willing to provide too much in the way of resources, or delegate too much in the way of authority, to their European-level associations. This is entirely sensible when ultimate political authority resides in the Council of Ministers. As Butt Philip (1985, p. 40) comments:

> Once the Council of Ministers assumes responsibility the national pressure groups take over from the Euro-groups. They then have to try to influence events by lobbying the various national ministries which will then have some say in determining their government's negotiating position in the Council. So the national members of each Euro-group cannot afford to devote too much responsibility for handling Community business to the Euro-group, since effective lobbying requires the national members to be actively engaged in bringing pressure to bear at other levels, and at times simultaneously.

## How European-level groups operate

Much of the attention of the European-level pressure groups is necessarily focused on the Commission or, more specifically, Commission services, the officials making up the various directorates-general. They also, however, make some use of contacts with the European Parliament and, to a lesser extent, the Economic and Social Committee. One general point that must be stressed is that the Commission is a very open bureaucracy compared to that of Britain, and pressure groups are allowed to exert influence at an even earlier stage of the decision-making process. The character of this atmosphere, and the reasons for it, were well explained in interview by the Brussels public affairs manager of a British multinational:

It is worth saying that the Commission is a more permeable and receptive body than a lot of people think. It goes back to a basic feature of its existence. It is a policy-making body, but not a democratic body. In Whitehall, a civil servant is really quite happy to talk, but he's looking over his shoulder at the minister, he's responsible to the minister, looking over his shoulder at the party the minister belongs to. Civil servants would say, 'It's nice to hear from you, but the policy is coming through.' At a certain moment [in the decision-making process] they will listen to representations. The EEC Commission does not have that grass roots link, it doesn't have any roots. The process of forming policies has to take place in some sort of framework. The Commission doesn't mind people knowing when something starts to be worked on, because it lets people know, then it gets some sort of imput.

In many ways, the lobbying atmosphere in Brussels is more reminiscent of Washington DC than of London. This can be seen in a number of ways. First, the public affairs managers of major companies in Brussels are involved in a significant way with the work of the relevant European-level trade associations in a manner similar to the role of government relations managers in Washington. In part, this reflects the fact that in both cases the company headquarters are usually some distance away, adding to the costs of participation for line managers. However, this difference is more than a question of convenience. In both cities there is a very fluid decision-making process which can move forward only through complex bargains. This leads to a greater emphasis on the professionalisation of the government relations function.

Just as in Washington, however, this professionalisation is accompanied by an informality of style. Much business is transacted over lunch or dinner. There is also an aggressive willingness to exploit any chance of building up contacts, for example through shared hobbies or sports, which is also reminiscent of Washington. There is also considerable use of lobbyists and consultants as intermediaries, particularly by interests who cannot justify full-time representation in Brussels (for example, English local authorities) or to undertake particular tasks for firms or associations (for example, monitoring the European Parliament).

Although various kinds of informal contact are important, much of the work of European-level pressure groups is taken up in routine contacts with Commission officials by telephone or at meetings. Table 5.4 provides information about CEFIC's main contacts in the European Commission. Some directorates-general will, of course, be more receptive to particular representations than others. Thus, DG VI (agriculture) has close contacts with agricultural groups; DG III (industrial

**Table 5.4** CEFIC's main EC Commission contacts

| Commissioners | | Chefs de cabinet | |
| --- | --- | --- | --- |
| DG I | External market | DG XII | R&D |
| DG III | Industrial affairs | DG XV | Taxation |
| DG IV | Competition | DG XVI | Regional policy |
| DG V | Social affairs | DG XVII | Energy policy |
| DG VI | Agriculture | Statistical Office | |
| DG VII | Transport | Customs Union Service | |
| DG XI | Environment | | |

affairs and internal market) acts in some respects as a sponsor for particular industries; and DG XI (environment) tends to see its mission as extending environmental protection, which provides a good basis for relations with environmental groups. Just as in Britain, there are interdepartmental battles betwen the various directorates-general, defining particular points of view which are often close to those of the client groups with which they are associated.

Contacts with individual commissioners are relatively infrequent, and may be less useful than regular contacts with officials engaged in the development of policy. One public affairs manager commented in interview:

> We have organised periodic state visits by the chairman plus one or more main board directors, really on what [the then chairman of company] calls a 'marmalade spreading' basis, to be nice to them, that we think they're important. Where we do have any issues where we want to get at commissioners, the fact of having this contact established is useful.

The same respondent stressed that 'The role of cabinets is absolutely key.' (Each commissioner has a small cabinet of officials serving him. At one time, they had the same nationality as the commissioner, but they are now of mixed origin.) In particular, he stressed the importance of the meeting of *chefs de cabinet* held before the weekly meeting of the Commission. He explained:

> Within each cabinet you have people who are dealing with all issues. Commissioners have to give views on all issues. If something goes through that you don't like, there's not much point in going to the cabinet of the commissioner presenting it. You have got to talk to someone in another cabinet so that they can ask awkward questions.

European-level groups do try and maintain contacts with the European Parliament but, as one association director commented in interview, 'It's a matter of priorities . . . If we had more staff, we could do something. They are a lower priority.' The Economic and Social Committee tends to be an even lower priority. One respondent commented, 'It's a weedy sort of organisation. My view of them yo-yos around a zero point. Sometimes I think it's worth no attention at all.' However, European-level interest groups will from time to time make an input on technical matters of concern to them.

## Direct contacts with Community institutions

Direct contacts with Community institutions are an important channel of access both for national pressure groups and for the public affairs managers of large firms in Brussels. One consequence of the difficulty of reaching agreements in European-level organisations is that national organisations make considerable use of separate representations to the Commission on their own behalf. An official of a British food industry pressure group has explained:

> There is no doubt that the national members of CIAA maintain their informal liaison with the Commission, particularly, but by no means exclusively, with those in the Cabinets of Commissioners and the directorate-generals of like nationality. FDIC [the Food and Drink Industries Council] maintains some direct links with Commission staff, indeed the latter have on occasion requested it, but it has been reluctant to detract from the authority of CIAA. On the other hand, CIAA is not always able to reach agreement, particularly on trading matters, so that if an organization feels it is insufficient to leave matters entirely in the hands of its national officials (who establish their own priorities) it has no other alternative than to have unofficial contact with the Commission.
> (Stocker 1983, p. 244)

The public affairs managers of major companies located in Brussels are necessarily engaged in developing direct contacts with Community institutions, an activity which sometimes concerns European-level federations who fear that their influence may be undermined. One public affairs manager commented in interview, 'On every issue you have to assess how to use different channels. On a big issue you use all of them . . . if you have a significant issue, you work it everywhere.' Another public affairs manager commented that the bulk of his contacts were with the commission. Matters being discussed by the Council of Ministers were primarily handled by London. However, the Council of Ministers secretariat could be useful in providing information about the progress being made on particular matters. He also had a role in relation to the UK permanent delegation, 'a useful body because they know what's going on, like a mini-Whitehall'.

A few major groups such as the 'CBI and NFU have set up offices in Brussels. These were often conceived primarily as listening posts and/or as service centres for national association members and staff attending meetings in Brussels. In the case of the CBI, the tasks of this office changed and developed during Britain's first decade of EC membership as CBI staff in London became more familiar with the operation of the Community. They were then able to take full responsibility for EC-related matters as an integrated part of their normal work.

The Community's official position has been 'to encourage the development of a European view of particular issues, rather than the separate articulation in Brussels of separate national viewpoints' (Butt Philip 1985, p. 9). In practice, however, direct contacts have continued between Commission officials and national pressure group representatives. Moreover, when particular European industries have been in crisis, the crucial meetings have often been direct ones between commissioners and heads of companies, albeit companies usually operating in more than one member state.

## The Seveso Directive

The complexity of the Community's decision-making processes makes it difficult to connect generalisations with specific examples. In order to illustrate the nature of the decision-making process, and the involvement of pressure groups in that process, two case studies are presented here: the evoltuion of the 'Seveso Directive' and the Labelling Directive of 1978.

In 1976 a chemical factory in Seveso, Italy, exploded. A cloud of TCDD, one of the most potent man-made toxins known, was released, and several villages had to be evacuated. Major incidents often lead to new environmental measures and the Italian catastrophe led the European Community to draw up a new Major Accidents Hazards Directive, more generally known as the 'Seveso Directive'. (Other major chemical accidents occurred at Bhopal in India in 1984; Basel in Switzerland in

1986; and Lyon and Nantes in France in 1987.) The Seveso Directive was finally adopted in December 1981 for implementation by December 1984. It set up a system for the notification of the most dangerous installations, together with a number of measures aimed at preventing accidents or mitigating their impact. The relevant British regulations came into force on 8 January 1985.

Such a long, drawn-out decision-making process clearly offers many opportunities for pressure groups to exert influence. While the Directive was being discussed, it was possible to exert influence both on the national governments of member states and the Eruopean Commission. The Health and Safety Executive, the body responsible for drawing up the British regulations, maintained close contacts with industrial pressure groups, issuing a formal consultation document and engaging in extensive informal discussions. For example, the Chemical Industries Association was 'fully involved in their development'. However, it was 'necessary to exert pressure to ensure that the [British] Regulation did not go beyond the requirements of the "Seveso" Directive' (CIA Activities Report 1985). The associations advised their members on how to implement the regulations, in particular in relation to arrangements for informing the public and the provision of off-site emergency plans.

Britain seems to have made more of an effort to implement the Directive than some other member states. By 1987 only four countries had incorporated the Directive in their national law. Moreover, the member states have interpreted some of the provisions in different ways, particularly in the importance attached to quantified risk analysis. Some aspects of the Directive still have to be developed, such as the use of accident reports for prevention purposes, a difficult task in which industry expertise will be required. CEFIC has already issued a paper on this subject.

By 1987 the Commission had started the process of revising the Directive in the light of experience. The first revision in March 1987 was concerned with correcting anomalies in the initial text. A second revision then focused on including isolated warehouses and stores. The Basel incident in 1986 had involved a fire in a storehouse. Although the incident occurred in Switzerland, it badly polluted the Rhine, killing an estimated half a million fish. In a few years' time, there will be a fundamental revision of the Directive. The policy-making process thus continues more than a decade after the original incident, involving consultation with pressure groups at the European and national levels.

## Labelling of food products

Labelling of food products is not an arcane question of little general concern, but a matter of considerable importance to consumers and manufacturers. Turner (1982, p. 27) notes that 'the marketing and selling of food is a fiercely competitive business and labels play an important part in promoting products'. The Food Labelling Directive was approved by the Council of Ministers in December 1978, but member states were given four years to implement the legislation, the relevant British regulations being introduced in January 1983. The Directive and subsequent regulations introduced a number of changes in good labelling, but among the more important were open date marking (the 'best before' date) and the identification of additives by their function and E number.

The first draft of the EEC Food Labelling Directive appeared in June 1974. During its slow passage through the decision-making process in Brussels, the then Food and Drink Industries Council (FDIC) 'played a most active part, in close co-operation with the Ministry [of Agriculture, Fisheries and Food], in helping to shape the Food Labelling Directive' (*FDIC Bulletin*, no. 21, p. 5). The Ministry kept a wide range of groups informed about the progress of the negotiations and its own negotiating stance, issuing four progress reports on discussions in the Council of Ministers' working group between September 1976 and January 1977 (Coates 1984, p. 154).

However, perhaps the most important role of the British pressure groups occurred at the stage of the drafting of the necessary regulations, when FDIC 'worked hand in hand with the Ministry' (*FDIC Bulletin*, no. 21, p. 5). Other organisations such as the Food Manufacturers Federation (FMF) were also involved in 'a continual process of assessing and interpreting the proposals, seeking clarification and submitting comments to MAFF' (MAFF Annual Report 1981, p. 26). One issue that arose was a concern that a prosecution for the new offence of misleading presentation created by the Directive could arise from the positioning of goods in a shop. The regulations were redrafted so that consumers have to be misled 'to a material degree' before there is a prosecution.

A particularly important development was the production in July 1981 of a guide to the new regulations, endorsed by the Ministry, enforcement officers, retailers and food industry associations. Consultations between civil servants and food industry associations led to significant amendments in the final version of this document. It does not have the force of law but, as it represents an agreement on provisions of the implementing regulations where difficulties of interpretation may arise, it is intended they should reduce the need to resort to the courts.

The FDIC also met with potentially opposed pressure groups. The Bureau of European Consumer Unions (BEUC) has been critical of the Directive. However, after a meeting between the FDIC's Labelling Working Group and BEUC it became apparent that BEUC's requirements for tighter control of labelling, particularly nutritional labelling, were less demanding than had been feared from their published statements.

This case study illustrates the intricate nature of the decision-making process arising from EC initiatives, and the extent to which Community and national dimensions are interwoven. The process is also one which never terminates. By 1987 the FDF (formed from a merger of the FDIC and the FMF) was engaged in discussions with MAFF about proposed amendments to the Labelling Directive. FDF was concerned, for example, that compulsory 'use before' labelling should be limited to microbiologically perishable foods.

## Conclusions

The discussion in this chapter has suggested that policy making in the Community is a highly complex, often technical and rather unpredictable process. Considerations of national interest remain important, but persistent obstructionism by one member state would be a self-defeating policy in the longer run. Hence, the decision-making process proceeds through the construction of complex bargains. Butt Philip (1985, p. 62) notes that a 'common outcome of disagreements in the Council ... is simply a watering-down of the Commission's proposals, sometimes to the point where there can seem little to be gained in continuing with them'. Clearly, pressure groups can benefit from such a watering-down process.

It must be emphasised, however, that the Community policy-making process is not a matter of producer groups halting or diluting proposals that affect the interests of their members. For example, the placing of E numbers on food labels contributed to increased public interest in additives (see Chapter 3). The environment directorate-general brings forward proposals which have a significant impact on environmental regulation in Europe. The Commission has provided financial support to the European Environmental Bureau.

The FDF noted in its 1986 annual report that the year 'saw an increase in the number of matters which affect our industry emanating from the EEC'. Other pressure groups, not just producer groups, are being affected in a similar way. The importance of European Community initiatives is likely to increase as 1992 approaches. One fear that has been expressed in neo-liberal circles is that the EC will reintroduce corporatism into Britain 'through the back door'. It is certainly the case that the EC attaches a greater importance to contacts with economic interest groups than is currently fashionable in Britain, particularly the so-called social partners (employers' organisations, unions, etc.). Following the Paris summit, the Commission set up a Bureau of Social Partners within the Secretariat-General of the Commission to facilitate consultation with social partner organisations. In general, however, 'At the Community level, there is relatively little evidence of the development of corporatist structures and functions' (Sargent, 1987, p. 252).

It is difficult to predict the future development of pressure group activities in relation to the European Community, given the uncertainties that surround the completion of the internal market and the difficulties that are likely to recur in relations between member states. One can say with some confidence that the European dimension is likely to be of increasing importance in the future, although it is more difficult to forecast the combinations of the three basic methods outlined here that British pressure groups will use to promote their interests. Certainly, future studies of all sectional, and some promotional, groups will have to include the European Community as a fundamental aspect of their analyses.

# 6

# The Effectiveness of Pressure Groups

Any study of pressure groups must be concerned not only with how they operate, but also with what they are able to achieve. Questions about who gains and who loses should be at the core of any political analysis. Two chapters will therefore be devoted to the analysis of the effectiveness of pressure groups. This chapter will be concerned with general questions about effectiveness. What are the methodological problems that arise in its study? What general factors can be discerned which help to explain the relative effectiveness or ineffectiveness of different pressure groups? Chapter 7 will present a case study of a particular policy area, agriculture and the environment. Agricultural pressure groups have generally been perceived as among the most effective in post-war Britain. Is that still the case? In particular, how have agricultural interests been influenced by the growing strength of the environmental movement?

Despite its importance, Whiteley and Winyard (1987, p. 111) note that 'the question of interest group effectiveness is probably the least adequately researched aspect of the study of pressure groups'. The principal reason is the methodological problems which arise in the analysis of effectiveness. More generally in the study of politics, we do not have any adequate means of measuring power and influence.

Indeed, the existence of two distinct terms — power and influence — itself hints at some of the problems. Without going into a complex conceptual debate, power may be said to refer to the exercise of authority ('legitimate power') by government and the deployment of coercive power by a non-governmental authority (such as a trade union). Both senses embody in them the notion of 'command', of obedience because one party either ought to be obeyed or has the ability to force the other party to obey/ Influence, on the other hand, rests on the power to persuade, and is the most usual way in which pressure groups are able to influence the decision-making process. Government makes concessions to a pressure group because of the validity of its arguments, for example because the group is able to demonstrate that the proposed policy is unworkable or would damage the economy, or because its arguments have moral force. Government and Parliament may also be influenced by the state of public opinion on the particular issue, although it must be stressed that the majority of issues discussed between pressure groups and government are of such a technical character that there is no public opinion in relation to them. /

## Why measuring pressure group influence is difficult

Even if the British political process were conducted in conditions of less secrecy, it would be difficult to estimate the effectiveness of a pressure group. The first problem arises from the objectives of the group itself. Some cause groups have relatively simple objectives, and it is possible to say whether or not they have been attained. Thus, the supporters of the abolition of capital punishment attained their objective (although whether for all time remains to be seen). The supporters of the abolition of hunting have yet to attain their objective (although banning hunting from particular tracts of land may be an intermediate step along the way).

Objectives may be clearly defined, but it may be uncertain whether group action has brought them about. CND would argue that it was popular pressure from itself and peace movements in other European countries that led to the 1987 treaty between the USA and the Soviet Union. Byrd argues that the treaty was negotiated over European heads to suit American interests. The outcome had little to do with the peace movement; even in the Netherlands, where the peace weapon was strongest, new weapons had been successfully deployed (Byrd 1988, p. 12). Popular pressure from the peace movement may, however, have reinforced other pressures to negotiate a solution to the intermediate nuclear weapons issue.

/ Matters become much more difficult when one considers sectional groups. Such groups have multiple objectives. Some of these objectives may matter a great deal to them, others much less so. Indeed, the complex internal politics of such groups may lead to policies being developed which are intended to appease some faction or interest within the group, but which are not really supported by the leadership. Obviously, such policies will not be pressed very hard. Even supposing, however, that it were possible to attach weights to the various policies being advocated by a group, one would still be left with the problem of measuring the degree of success attained.

Occasionally, a sectional group gets all that it wants on a particular issue. For much of the time, however, it has to agree to a compromise. The compromise may be a bad one from the group's point of view, yet the group leadership may put a gloss on it to calm the membership. Equally, the compromise may be quite a favourable one, but the group may complain loudly about the harshness of its treatment, largely for the consumption of its membership. Even trying to trace the real impact of the compromise on the group's members may be very difficult, as much will depend on its implementation. There are many provisions on the statute book which are hardly ever used.

There are also problems in deciding what government's priorities really are. Sometimes government may 'toughen up' a Green Paper or a White Paper so that it has something to give away to pressure groups at a later stage without compromising its core position (although this was a more frequent tactic in the 1970s when governments were less determined and less politically secure). Policy also often emerges as a series of compromises produced on the basis of interdepartmental arguments, with each department frequently arguing for the client groups with which it is associated.

In any case, how does one compare a substantial impact on a policy which is basically unfavourable to a group with some small adjustments to a policy which is more in line with a group's thinking? This is not a purely academic issue. The CBI had much more influence on the policy of the Labour Government of 1974—9 than it did on the policies of the preceding and succeeding Conservative governments. However, the policy proposals of the Labour Government were potentially more threatening to the CBI's interests than those of the Conservatives. The position is further complicated by the fact that members of the Labour Government were either opposed to particular policies (substantial intervention in industry) or unenthusiastic about them (industrial democracy). Hence, the CBI was a useful ally for the more moderate members of the Government in their internal policy struggles.

If one considers the interaction betwen pressure groups and government, it is relatively rare for only one group to be active on a particular issue. A number of groups will be taking a variety of positions, and using different strategies. For example, both the Church of England and the Roman Catholic Church successfully opposed the introduction of charges for school transport. However, 'Those of us negotiating on behalf of the Church of England were not happy with the Roman Catholic representatives' narrow view of free or subsidized transport' (Waddington 1985, p. 248). Moreover, 'the clause on charges for transport was not in our opinion an issue on which we would choose to mount all our forces of opposition' (p. 250). The Church of England considered that there might be more fundamental educational issues in the future which would require it to use its trump cards. They therefore concentrated on low-key lobbying of the DES. By contrast, the Roman Catholics ' "pulled out all the stops", with interventions ranging from a *démarche* by Cardinal Hulme to the application to Roman Catholic peers of what was, effectively, a "three-line whip" ' (Medhurst and Moyser 1988, p. 332). Who is to say which approach was the more effective? Indeed, the deciding factor might have been an intervention in the House of Lords by Lord Butler, the architect of the 1944 Education Act.

There may also be instances when an apparent failure in the short term may have more beneficial consequences in the longer term, at least in terms of establishing the issue on the policy agenda. The Church of England waged an unsuccessful campaign against the 1981 Nationality Act. However, despite the failure to prevent the legislation being enacted:

> there are indications that the original campaign, and subsequent aid to individuals, have increased awareness of the issue both inside and outside the Church. Indeed, the General Synod was persuaded roundly to repudiate the Nationality Act, to the possible embarrassment of Conservative parliamentarians in its midst. The result may be an enlarged body of supportive opinion that could be mobilized in subsequent campaigns.
>
> (Medhurst and Moyser 1988, p. 343)

Whiteley and Winyard (1987, p. 111) suggest that 'a second-best solution to observing the decision-making process directly' is to interview participants and obtain their perceptions of effectiveness. Much useful data can be obtained in this way, although large-scale studies of this kind (such as have been carried out in the United States) are expensive and would need to be repeated from time to time to capture changing perceptions. In the rest of this chapter, an attempt is made to isolate the more important factors which might affect the effectiveness of a pressure group.

## A typology of factors affecting pressure group effectiveness

The following typology draws on a number of sources in the pressure group literature. Among the most influential have been Presthus (1973, 1974); Schmitter and Streeck (1981), and the literature of the Organisation of Business Interests project in general; and Whiteley and Winyard (1987).

The typology is divided into three main categories which are then subdivided into subsidiary headings:

1. Features of the proximate environment of groups, the 'domains' they are seeking to organise. In particular:
   (i) the characteristics of the potential membership being organised or represented;
   (ii) competition between groups for members and influence.

2. The resources available to groups:
   (i) internal group structures such as decision-taking and conflict resolution mechanisms;
   (ii) financial resources;
   (iii) staff resources;
   (iv) membership mobilisation capabilities;
   (v) sanctioning capacity;
   (vi) choices of strategy.

3. Features of the external economic and political environment:
   (i) public opinion/attitudes;
   (ii) the political party in office;
   (iii) economic circumstances;
   (iv) delegated authority.

The rest of the chapter will be structured around a consideration of these various points.

### Domain organisation

Schmitter and Streeck (1981, pp. 146–7) observe:

> The most basic decision in the design of an interest association is to select from the variety of existing interests those which the association will represent, and to institutionalize a distinction between these and other interests whose representation is left to other associations. Interest associations define the interests they choose to internalize by formally demarcating an organizational *domain*.

In other words, pressure groups will decide whom it is they are seeking to represent, and this decision will be reflected in criteria of membership eligibility set out in their constitution. Of course, membership of some cause groups is open to the population at large. For all sectional groups, however, membership is limited in some way. Among cause groups, some may draw their members from a particular disadvantaged category, while others may be made up of concerned individuals seeking to remedy the problems of those in the disadvantaged category. Whiteley and Winyard (1987, p. 27) formalise this distinction, considering promotional groups as those 'that speak on behalf of, or *for* the poor, while representational groups are those whose membership is made up *of* the poor, or a particular category of claimant'.

Interestingly, Whiteley and Winyard found that, if anything, the promotional groups were more effective than the representational groups. This appeared to be because the representational groups were not seen by civil servants as truly representative of their categories, or able to deliver their clienteles, while the promotional groups displayed more professional expertise in pressure group activity (pp. 132–3). Another relevant factor appeared to be the 'attractiveness' of the client group in terms of its electoral influence and the degree to which it was seen as 'deserving'. 'It is easier to arouse public concern and the support of decision makers for the elderly than for, say, offenders or the low paid' (p. 131).

It is important for a group with a restricted eligible membership to organise as large a proportion of it as possible in order to be credible. Trade associations will often claim with pride that they represent 93 per cent of the firms in terms of sales or employment in the widget industry or whatever sector they are organising. Indeed, Presthus (1974, p. 111) argues that 'size and quality of membership are probably among the major political resources of interest groups'. Cause groups in Britain tend to attract a disproportionate number of well-educated, middle-class members. For example, the available evidence suggests that 'members of environmental groups are predominantly middle class' (Lowe and Goyder 1983, p. 10). Such individuals tend to have high levels of self-confidence and to be articulate, good at drafting papers, knowledgeable about the political system and able to hold their own in meetings with officials.

In practice, there is considerable overlap between the domains of pressure groups. Sometimes, this overlap is accidental. For example, the structure of trade associations in Britain has grown in an *ad hoc* basis over a hundred years or so, and is consequently beset by a lack of coherence in the division of responsibilities. Sometimes, however, overlaps may reflect differences of interest. For example, the construction industry has a large number of associations representing, for example, large firms and small firms, contractors and subcontractors, civil engineers and builders, etc. To some extent, each of these associations could be said to be representing distinct domains. However, it is clear that some of the associations are competing for members and influence, leading to a situation in which government has a series of voices claiming to speak for the industry. West Germany has a much more coherent structure of associations in the industry (see Grant and Streeck 1985).

Such competition for members and influence is not limited to sectional groups. Cause groups may be divided along such lines as the tactics to be used to further a shared objective, as, for example, with the anti-hunting lobby. In the disability field, 'There has been considerable rivalry between the Disablement Income Group, the Royal Association for Disability and Rehabilitation and the Disability Alliance' (Whiteley and Winyard 1987, p. 134). In this instance, the influence of particular individuals appears to be one factor in perpetuating the divisions.

If groups representing a potentially homogeneous category of interest are divided, then government has the option of using a 'divide and rule' strategy. Such a strategy was in evidence in the nurses' dispute in 1988 when the Government indicated its willingness to talk to the moderate Royal College of Nursing, whilst refusing to talk to COHSE and NUPE while they continued to use disruptive tactics. However, even leaving aside ideologically based disagreements about strategies and tactics, it is not necessarily easy for groups to 'get together' and present a united front. A merger or joint action may be more in the interests of one group than another. Coates makes it clear in his study of the teaching unions that the National Union of Teachers (NUT) had the most to gain from organisational unity:

> The impetus for the creation of a single teachers' organisation has come always from the largest association, the NUT ... Lack of unity, in the Union's view, dissipated the potential for influence that the teachers collectively possessed through the traditional forms of their pressure. And, of course, as the largest of the associations by far, the NUT had the most to gain from the creation of an organisational unit that it would inevitably dominate, and in which sectional voices would be muted.
>
> (Coates 1972, p. 47)

It is not surprising that, over fifteen years later, the teaching unions remain divided with one new organisation being added to the total, the anti-strike Professional Association of Teachers. It is arguable that one of the factors leading to poor industrial relations in the schools has been competition for members between the different unions.

Equally, it is clear that, where pressure groups have been able to supplant competitors, this has been an important source of strength. Before the Second World War, 'the influence of farmers on agricultural policy was not strong', one reason being that 'In the thirties the National Farmers' Union (NFU) was only one of several agricultural pressure groups . . . trying to influence Government' (Smith 1988, p. 5).

Interests which appear at first sight to be homogeneous and united may on closer inspection turn out to be more fragmented and divided. This is apparent, for example, from Moran's work on the financial services sector (or the 'City of London' as it is often, rather inaccurately, called). 'The most casual observation soon dispels the illusion that there exists in the City either a community of interests or agreement on tactics' (Moran 1983, p. 5). Changes in the financial services sector, such as the removal of old barriers between different types of business, the emergence of financial conglomerates, and the end of trading on the floor of the Stock Exchange, have eroded the old social unity of the City. The opening up of new areas of competition between, for example, clearing banks and building societies has implications for patterns of political representation. The old pattern of the Governor of the Bank of England conveying the 'City view' to the Chancellor or Prime Minister has been largely supplanted by the emergence of professionalised trade associations representing different segments of the financial services sector.

### Resources: internal group structures

One of the ways in which the NFU has reduced external competition is by having an internal structure in which a variety of viewpoints (according to different commodities, different types of land, etc.) can be fed into the organisation's decision-making process. Similar devices are employed by many trade associations, for example special committees or reserved seats on the main decision-making body for small-firm members who may otherwise feel excluded by larger members.

Despite the usefulness of devices of this kind, there is a difficult trade-off between a widely based organisation with a large membership but significant internal tensions, and an organisation with a small, but tightly knit membership. It is sometimes said, for instance, that the CBI suffers from 'stifling breadth' because it attempts to represent small and large firms; manufacturers, financiers and retailers; nationalised industries and private sector firms; importers and exporters, etc. It is clear that 'A central problem in the design of associational structures is the management of internal interest diversity' (Schmitter and Streeck 1981, p. 142). Highly publicised 'exits' of members (as has happened in the CBI) and the formation of breakaway organisations (as has happened in the NFU) can be damaging to an organisation's reputation. On the other hand, the price of preventing such splits may be a high one in terms of the quality of the policies produced and their impact on government.

Pressure groups have to develop decision-making structures which take account of the different interests and viewpoints of their members whilst being able to develop effective policies and to respond to changing events. In many sectional groups, a typical pattern is to have a large council which is the ultimate decision-making body but which only really takes decisions in situations where significant sections of the membership are offended by a policy proposal. An executive committee is often in effective charge of the overall strategy of the organisation. Much of the real work, however, is done by a series of specialised committees dealing with particular problem areas. These may, in turn, spawn working parties to deal with a particular piece of legislation or EC directive. Co-ordinating the work of these various committees, and keeping the overall committee structure under review, is one of the tasks of the professional staffs of the associations.

Cause groups may have a more straightforward structure, with considerable responsibility falling both on the executive committee collectively and on its individual members, whose particular responsibilities serve as the functional equivalent of specialised committees in sectional groups. Many cause groups have a relatively decentralised structure, often for ideological reasons. Such structures have their advantages and disadvantages. They involve members in local protest actions which are often seen by cause groups as an important part of their work. They can feed back information on how government policies are working in practice on the ground. Whiteley and Winyard's research shows that civil servants valued information from pressure groups on how the social security system was working in practice so that shortcomings could be identified and rectified (1987, pp. 131–2). On the other hand, a decentralised structure may lead to local groups taking actions which contradict group policy or embarrass the group and make its relations with civil servants more difficult. In a decentralised organisation, the centre may be starved of the financial resources it requires to function effectively.

## Financial resources and staff size

Financial resources are important to a group in the sense that if it is going to engage in the detailed monitoring of legislation (including EC directives), and attempt to influence the content of such legislation through the presentation of a detailed case to civil servants, it will require a large, relatively well-paid staff. As Moran (1983, p. 51) observes, 'The characteristic way in which powerful interests have influenced policy-making in modern Britain may be summarised in one word: they have done so *bureaucratically.*' Having interviewed many pressure group officials over the years, one of the most striking characteristics of most of them is their similarity to civil servants in terms of their official personalities, modes of operation, language, and perceptions of the political process. After all, they are civil servants, preparing policy papers for and generally servicing committees, and making presentations to their counterparts in government. Such skills have to be developed by cause groups, just as much as by sectional groups, if they want to be effective. In the case of the poverty lobby, 'Officials and politicians saw group effectiveness in terms of the quality of the information provided' (Whiteley and Winyard 1987, p. 122).

Buksti and Johansen suggest on the basis of Danish research that the size of the secretariat or bureaucracy of an organisation is an important determinant of group effectiveness. They characterise organisations with fewer than six people on their staff as 'weak insiders' (1979, pp. 209–10). A rather similar view was taken by the Devlin Commission on Industrial Representation, which suggested that an effective association should have an executive staff of at least eight people.

This view does, however, need some qualification. For example, a product-level association which has to consider particular EC directives can operate quite effectively with a part-time executive officer shared with other similar associations and operating out of the offices of the sectoral association (a pattern adopted in the chemical and food-processing industries, for example). At the other end of the spectrum, there is a danger that a large association bureaucracy will develop objectives of its own which are at variance with those of the members. Indeed, one argument that has been put to me in an interview is that a small secretariat of a few very well-paid executives concentrating on major issues can work just as well as an association with large numbers of middle-ranking officials scrutinising the details of policy, although in practice such details can be very significant.

One also has to consider the calibre of the staff themselves. What qualities are required of pressure group officials? Some associations like to recruit from the industry they represent, which may be sensible if the association's work has a substantial technical content. Occasionally, high-ranking civil servants nearing retirement are recuited to head an association on the realistic assumption that they will know their way around the corridors of Whitehall. Some associations like to recruit retired military personnel to staff their organisations, but in some cases this has had disastrous consequences, given that pressure groups are complex organisations which do not respond to instructions in the same way as military subordinates. An increasing trend in recent years has been the emergence of the pressure group professional who is recognised as having a collection of skills which can be transferred from one organisation to another (this is particularly applicable to trade associations, but instances have also occurred among cause groups). However, there is no real profession of 'association management', as there is no real specialised training and no professional examinations.

Financial resources are often important if a pressure group is to be influential in the long run, as distinct from having a 'one-off' success resulting from riding a tide in public opinion. However, it should be noted that there are instances of pressure groups with small secretariats being influential, either because their co-operation was seen as important to the attainment of government policy objectives, or because they possessed resources of expertise among their members.

An example of a group gaining stature because of government policy is provided by the Retail Consortium in the 1970s. The Retail Consortium is the 'umbrella' organisation for the retail sector, staffed by a small secretariat. In the 1970s, under Conservative and Labour governments, the restraint of retail prices was a major policy objective. Hence, the Retail Consortium was given the rare privilege of access to the Chancellor and Prime Minister. The relationship reached its most intense with the so-called 'red triangle' scheme, operated with the co-operation of the Retail Consortium, which aimed to limit prices on certain basic foodstuffs. With the end of price controls, the Retail Consortium reverted to a less exalted status. When it asked to meet the Chancellor in 1981, it was told he could not find the time to see the group's representatives.

The Nationalised Industry Chairmen's Group (NICG) has had access to the highest levels of government in spite of the fact that it has been serviced by a secretariat of only seven executives, six of them seconded from member industries. The NICG has always taken the view that it would be wrong to build up a large secretariat. Its principal strength has been the fact that it has comprised the heads of the principal nationalised industries. In addition, it has been able to draw on the expertise of specialist panels made up of senior managers, such as that bringing together the chief economic advisers of the nationalised industries. Even under the Conservatives, the NICG has been influential, forestalling Government proposals for stricter controls over the remaining public corporations.

### Membership mobilisation and sanctioning capacity

The ability to mobilise the membership in support of a particular campaign can be a useful resource, especially for cause groups seeking to attract media attention. Groups such as the Hunt Saboteurs Association which use 'direct action' techniques clearly rely on the active participation of members. Nearly a third of the members attend demonstrations (Thomas 1983, p. 159). Mobilisation is a rather different matter for sectional pressure groups, although the CBI did attempt to develop the notion of 'employer solidarity' in the late 1970s. In 1978 the CBI persuaded its members to refuse to sign new government contracts containing a clause requiring adherence to the Government's pay policies. Although the CBI President of the day claimed that 'this cohesion can be seen as a most important milestone on the road to improved employer solidarity' (CBI Annual Report 1978, p. 3), the drive for employer solidarity fizzled out, particularly after the failure of a scheme to provide strike insurance for CBI members.

There are some pressure groups which have sanctioning capacity in the sense that they are able to take actions that force government to modify or reverse its policies. A clear example is strike action by a trade union. In the 1970s, strikes took on an increasingly political hue, often because they were in industries where government was the employer, but also because incomes policies tended to politicise conventional industrial disputes. The most successful political strike during this period, however, was that co-ordinated by the Ulster Workers' Council which paralysed Northern Ireland for two weeks in May 1974, bringing down the 'power sharing' executive after only five months in office.

The widespread use of the strike weapon culminated in the 'winter of discontent' of 1978−9 (as so often, Shakespeare was plundered for an appropriate phrase to describe these events). If nothing else, Mr Callaghan's winter of discontent led to a glorious summer for Mrs Thatcher in which her brow was bound with victorious wreaths. When the Government used state power to crush a number of strikes, notably that of the miners, in the 1980s, there was little reaction from the public at large, fed up with being inconvenienced by unions who showed little or no concern for consumers. The misuse of the strike weapon thus rebounded on the unions, although the blame must be shared by the Labour Government for its mismanagement of the events of 1978−9.

The City of London has also been seen to have considerable sanctioning power with its ability to engage in a 'gilt-edged strike' (by refusing to buy government stock) or to 'talk down' sterling because of unease about government policy. The former sanction is, of course, of less value when there is a budget surplus and the government is actually buying back gilt-edged stock. A future Labour government might well find itself constrained by the reaction of the financial markets. However, given the internationalisation of financial markets, and the fragmentation of the City, this would be more a question of a change in market 'sentiment' than an organised political action. In any case, as Moran (1983, pp. 53−4) has pointed out:

> The City's great power was elusive because it rested, not on the crude capacity to influence overt policy, but on the fact that issues vital to the interests of financial markets . . . had become 'non-decisions': they were matters not thought to be the concern of bureaucratic politics in Whitehall or partisan politics in Westminster

## The choice of strategy

The choice of an appropriate strategy and tactics can be an important determinant of pressure group success, although there is a sense in which the adoption of unsophisticated strategies may be a reflection of ineffectiveness rather than its cause. Whiteley and Winyard (1987, p. 136) conclude:

> A quiet insider strategy does not pay off any better than an open promotional strategy. Since the era of consensus politics described by Beer and Eckstein, policy making has become more conflictual, but also more fragmented.

Whiteley and Winyard's research shows that the responsible use of publicity by a group can reinforce the lobbying of government. It is also apparent that there are more opportunities for exerting influence through Parliament than was the case in the 1950s when the first empirical pressure group studies were undertaken. Even so, it is clear that much success in lobbying still depends on the careful research and analysis of a case, and its presentation to civil servants. In that sense, the lobbying process remains a highly bureaucratised one in which adequate resources are one of the keys to success. Being too sophisticated can, however, be counterproductive. 'The much vaunted British Airways parliamentary lobby, so carefully and skilfully constructed since 1984, is now so slick that Ministers expect it and discount accordingly' (Miller 1988).

### External environment

Public attitudes and opinions are an important feature of the external operating environment of groups. A pressure group will usually try and influence public opinion. Although such efforts may have some success, groups are more likely to benefit from a change in public views which they have not themselves brought about. An important distinction can be made between 'attitudes' and 'opinions'. It will not be possible to discuss the literature on this subject here. For the purposes of this analysis, 'attitudes' are taken to refer to more deeply held perceptions which structure the response of individuals to particular events. They generally change only either slowly or in response to some crisis situation. Opinions are more superficial; they may reflect more deeply held attitudes, but they may also be more spontaneous responses to particular events.

As Richard Rose (1974, p. 253) points out, 'The likelihood of any group gaining wide popular support for its demands depends upon the congruence between group demands and the values, beliefs and emotions widely diffused in the culture.' Rose (pp. 254–5) develops a sixfold typology based on the level of congruence between a group's goals and wider cultural norms:

1. 'Harmony between pressure group demands and general cultural norms.' Rose gives the example of the Royal Society for the Prevention of Cruelty to Animals, which is able to draw on general public concern for animals.
2. 'A gradual increase in the acceptability of political values

supporting pressure group demands.' The example Rose gave in 1974, 'permissiveness' in the arts and in life styles, was valid at the time. A better example today might be anti-smoking groups, which Rose cites later as an example of public indifference. This is not to criticise Rose's choices, but rather to make the point that public attitudes do change over time in a way that impacts on group effectiveness.

3. 'Bargaining with fluctuating support from cultural norms.' Rose's example of the unions is an appropriate one. For such a group, strategies should be tailored to the circumstances it faces, being more defensive at some times than others.

4. 'Advocacy in the face of cultural indifference.' Such a group lacks an audience either in government or outside of it. The Pedestrians Association is a good example to replace that given by Rose. Despite the title of its journal, *Arrive*, this is an organisation that has never got there. It has only six hundred individual members, and is weak compared with the motoring organisations which are sustained by a general cultural fascination with the motor car.

5. 'Advocacy in opposition to long-term cultural trends.' Rose gives the Lord's Day Observance Society as an example of a group fighting a holding operation. Sunday trading laws have not been reformed, however, in part because they have also been opposed by pressure groups with other motives, such as the union representing retail workers.

6. 'Conflict between cultural values and pressure group goals.' Rose argues that groups such as pacifists cannot reach a bargained compromise because of their 'all or nothing' goals. Groups working for disarmament may, however, contribute to a climate of opinion in which world leaders are more willing to seek reconciliation of their differences.

As well as the popularity of the cause itself, attention must be paid to the impact on public opinion of the methods used. Rose refers to the harmony between groups working for animal welfare and general cultural norms. However, public opinion may be most tolerant of the 'respectable' methods of the RSPCA; less supportive of the hunt saboteurs; and opposed to the methods used by animal liberationists.

The importance of public opinion in setting a context for pressure group activity can be seen by the way in which the environmental movement has gained ground in the 1970s and 1980s. There is a risk, however, in such an increase in issue salience. Politicians may be tempted to jump on the bandwagon and make tokenistic commitments to the environmentalist cause. Environmental issues are particularly attractive to politicians seeking new ways of mobilising support because they do not generally involve large sums of public expenditure, rather the imposition of new regulations on business. It could be argued that there has been such a 'token' response by some politicians in Britain in the 1980s. Porritt and Winner (1988, p. 85) argue that 'the overwhelming majority of British politicians have barely begun to address the more radical challenges of green thinking'.

### The difference made by the party in office

The party in office can make a considerable difference to the political influence exerted by a pressure group. It must be emphasised that two governments with the same party label can be very different in their approach to pressure group activity. The Heath Government tried to develop a close working relationship with the trade unions, while the Thatcher Government was keen to distance itself from them. The personal preferences of the prime minister may be very significant. For example, the then head of the civil service recalled that Heath 'was often rude to the CBI — he thought they talked rubbish' (Holmes 1982, p. 51).

The TUC was the pressure group most adversely affected by the advent of the Thatcher Government. Using detailed data from TUC annual reports, Mitchell (1987) shows that the number of contacts at prime ministerial level fell off sharply after 1979, although ministerial contacts remained at the same level as under the Labour Government of 1974–9. What changed even more dramatically was the effectiveness of contacts as perceived by the TUC. Between 1976 and 1979, the success rate (in terms of government agreeing to take the action advocated by the TUC) varied between 40.5 per cent and 47.0 per cent. In the years from 1979 to 1984, it ranged between 4.5 per cent and 22.5 per cent, a striking contrast with the earlier period.

The poverty lobby has also been affected by the political climate of the 1980s. 'In the Thatcherite era of conviction politics the influence of poverty groups has been reduced by the ideological beliefs of that administration, and by the deteriorating economic climate that monetarist policies have created' (Whiteley and Winyard 1987, p. 138). The poverty lobby itself has been very resilient, with an increase in the number of groups, the interests covered, and the alliances between them. The membership of the CPAG doubled in the six years to 1988 (see Brynin 1988). Whiteley and Winyard provide an interesting review of the strategies open to the lobby, arguing that appeals to altruism are not enough, and that questions of allocative efficiency have to be addressed. They note (1987, p. 148) that 'unless an appeal can be made to a wider electorate based on self-interest rather than moral indignation, redistribution is never going to rally sufficient support to make real progress'.

In noting the changes brought about by Thatcherism, it is easy to ignore the continuities. Mrs Thatcher has been reluctant to make changes in the structure of government and, if anything, the issue communities organised around government departments have become more solidified in the 1980s. One of the key and enduring features of the British political process is the symbiotic relationship between groups and departments. The groups need the department for access, status, and information about policy developments; the departments need the groups for information about what is happening in their sphere of interest, for co-operation in the implementation of policy and, above all, as allies in the interdepartmental battles which are another key feature of the British political process. As new ministerial responsibilities emerge, new alliances are developed. Thus, when William Waldegrave was 'green' minister, the environmental groups 'were only too happy to play along with the game which he invited them to join, enlisting them as supporters of the department in the battles which they had to fight against other Government departments, particulary the Ministry of Agriculture' (Porritt and Winner 1988, p. 85).

In the next chapter, an example of a relationship between a ministry and its client group which has proved very beneficial to the pressure group, that between the Ministry of Agriculture and the NFU, will be analysed. There are, however, limits to what can be achieved within a particular issue community. There are interventions from the centre of government, from Downing Street and, more frequently, from the Treasury. Policy communities may also be fragmented within themselves. Thus, Whiteley and Winyard (1987, p. 127) observe that the extent to which groups are able to exert influence is 'vitiated by the degree of fragmentation both within central government and within the social security issue-community'.

Economic circumstances may have an impact on government's willingness to meet pressure group demands. Against a background of cutbacks in public expenditure, demands for increases in service provision, or other changes in policy requiring more expenditure, are unlikely to be met. However, what is important is the 'interaction between economic constraints and political priorities' (p. 126). By the late 1980s, government was running a substantial budget surplus but, consistent with its general policy priorities and its emphasis on 'sound money', the Government did not start to reverse earlier cutbacks in public expenditure. The budget surplus and a large contingency reserve did, however, give the Government considerable room for manoeuvre in meeting particular crises where a group's demands won considerable public sympathy, as with the nurses.

### Delegating implementation to pressure groups

Although this is less common in Britain than in countries such as West Germany, government often shares its authority with pressure groups, delegating to them the responsibility for carrying out particular functions, or providing particular services. Although this reliance on 'private interest governments' may seem to be a corporatist trait, its use has tended to increase under the Thatcher Government. Examples include the provision of training funds through non-statutory training organisations (effectively employers' associations), which replaced the former statutory training boards in most sectors of the economy and are to be extended to the remaining areas covered by statutory boards; the creation of self-regulatory organisations in the City of London with considerable disciplinary powers, including the ability to impose substantial fines; the involvement of the chambers of commerce in a number of government programmes; and the increased use of the voluntary sector for service delivery at the local level.

It is more difficult to decide what the impact of these new responsibilities is on the traditional lobbying role of the pressure groups. They do enhance the attractiveness of group membership, for example some employers' associations have advertised non-statutory training organisations as an additional selective benefit for their members. Administering the various functions does create new linkages with government. On the other hand, there is a risk of the groups being co-opted into government and losing their independence, while those groups that exercise delegated disciplinary powers may encounter resentment about the use of the powers among some of their members.

## Conclusions

An attempt has been made in this chapter to generalise about the factors affecting pressure group effectiveness. Although there are clearly some observable regularities in the ways in which successful groups operate, it must be emphasised that each pressure group faces a different situation, and has to develop and deploy a strategy to suit its particular circumstances.

Consider the example of the Society of Teachers Opposed to Physical Punishment (STOPP). Over twenty years after the group was formed in 1966, corporal punishment was banned in 1987 in state schools and for state-financed pupils in independent schools. The House of Commons accepted a House of Lords amendment abolishing corporal punishment on a free vote by 231 votes to 230 in 1986. STOPP thus attained its objective and was dissolved.

When STOPP was formed it faced an unpromising situation, including considerable hostility within schools. Its strategy was based first on ensuring that there could be no accusations of extremism, with its sponsors including a Conservative MP, a public school headmaster, and well-known peers. It kept to its single issue, refusing to become involved in wider educational controversies. It tried to change the language in which the debate about the issue was conducted. A founder member commented, 'Corporal punishment sounded like a respectable professional practice ... We talked about child beating' (*Independent*, 24 November 1988). A press cutting agency was used so that any reference to corporal punishment even in an obscure newspaper was followed up with a letter. Great care was taken over research to counteract claims that caning was in decline. 'It came to the point where we knew more about what was happening than anybody in the Department of Education' (*Independent*, 24 November 1988).

Some London education authorities banned corporal punishment in the 1970s. In 1980 the Labour and Liberal party conferences voted for abolition. In 1982 the NUT passed a resolution against corporal punishment in schools, followed in 1983 by the head teachers' associations. Even more significant, in 1982 the European Court found the UK guilty of breaching the European Convention by not respecting parental objections to corporal punishment. The Government then faced the prospect of paying compensation, so it introduced a bill allowing parents to opt their children out of corporal punishment. This bill was widely ridiculed and was subsequently withdrawn, leading to the final successful vote in 1986.

STOPP thus used a combination of methods. It was helped by having one clear objective, but it also seems to have been very careful in its choice of an appropriate strategy and tactics. It was firm, informed and persuasive without being hysterical or fanatical. Any group that wishes to be successful should bear these lessons in mind. There is always room for improvement: a survey of ministers, MPs and civil servants found that government at all levels was dissatisfied with the quality of lobbying (Public Policy Consultants 1987, p. 4).

Claus Offe has made an interesting distinction between groups which may be able to destabilise the social and political order and 'are able to influence the state by directly making demands on policy makers' and 'policy takers . . . whose members are *directly affected by* state policies' (Offe 1981, p. 138). The former category would include, for example, business associations; the latter, the poverty lobby. This is an interesting distinction which suggests that there are inherent inequalities in the distribution of power among pressure groups. Offe, however, probably places too much emphasis on the power of economic obstruction as distinct from more subtle methods of exerting influence. He maintains (p. 146) that 'The power of economic obstruction distinguishes labor and capital from traditional middle-class interests and interest groups, such as farmers and shopkeepers.' In the next chapter it will be argued that the farmers have been a relatively influential interest in Britain.

# 7

# Groups in Action: A Case Study of Agriculture and the Environment

In December 1988 the central focus of British political discussion was a row about alleged salmonella contamination of egg production. Press coverage of developing events included stories with headlines like 'Political change erodes the farmers' influence on the Tory Party' and 'The decline of the farming lobby'. The press coverage was echoed in the titles of academic analyses appearing in the late 1980s: *Farmers and the State: A Crisis for Corporatism?* or *Agriculture and Conservation in Britain: A Policy Community under Siege.* Three of the best-known analysts of the politics of agricultural policy commented, 'The sector's preferred and long regularised arrangements are being scrutinised and their rationale questioned in a manner hitherto unprecedented in the post-war period' (Cox *et al.* 1986b, p. 209).

But was the agricultural lobby really losing its considerable influence, or was it simply having to adapt its tactics to meet a new situation, adopting new policies and co-opting a wider range of interests? After all, the eggs crisis, which took the form of a classic interdepartmental battle between the agricultural and health ministries, ended with the resignation of the junior health minister whose remarks had triggered off the public debate, Mrs Edwina Currie, and with a government scheme to compensate egg producers. This chapter, then, is concerned with explaining the origins of the political influence of the agricultural lobby, and exploring the extent to which it has lost political ground — and, if so, why. This latter question will in part be explored in relation to

133

the extent to which the environmental lobby has been able to make progress on agricultural issues.

## The success of the agricultural lobby

There is no lack of evidence to suggest that the agricultural lobby has been successful in the past. This evidence may be summarised under three headings: 'exceptionalism'; subsidies and protection; and autonomy. Before exploring the evidence in more detail, it should be noted that Britain is not unusual in making general provision for agriculture. The United States, for example, gives considerable assistance to agriculture. Indeed, the Organisation for Economic Co-operation and Development calculated that the cost of supporting agriculture in member states nearly doubled between 1979–81 and 1986, reaching a level of around 200 billion ECU (£132 billion) in the latter year (*Financial Times*, 17 May 1988).

The notion of 'exceptionalism', developed in the work of Cox, Lowe and Winter, refers to the extent to which agriculture is exempted from many of the laws applying to other industries, and also has special provisions made for it. For example, agriculture is the only industry that is exempt from paying rates. Normal planning controls do not apply to farming. Indeed, farming has special arrangements across the whole range of environmental regulation:

> special voluntary arrangements or procedures, quite distinct from the statutory regulations imposed on other industries have evolved, as for example the Pesticides Safety Precautions Scheme. Indeed, the place of formal controls has tended to be taken by codes of conduct such as the NFU's Codes of Practice on Straw Burning, Aerial Spraying and Silage Effluent.
>
> (Cox *et al.* 1985, p. 145)

Further evidence of 'exceptionalism' can be found in the existence of a separate system of education for agriculture (agricultural colleges) which has no parallel in other industries, and the development of an extensive technical advice service for farmers, the Agricultural Development and Advisory Service (ADAS). Until recently, its services were generally provided free of charge. Corresponding provision in manufacturing industry, for example through research associations, has been comparatively limited.

Subsidies and trade protection for agriculture are proportionately greater than for any other industry. British membership of the European Community has seen a change in the way in which subsidies are provided, from a system of deficiency payments to a system of intervention purchasing or surplus production. The burden of support is thus shifted from the taxpayer to the consumer, but the farmer continues to be supported. Protection against external (to the EC) competition has been strengthened with, for example, the amount of New Zealand butter allowed into the British market being steadily reduced. Admittedly, in the recent past, there have been some reductions both in the level of grant aid provided by the British Government, and in the level of Community support for surplus production. However, new schemes have been introduced such as that for 'set aside' (paying farmers not to grow crops), and the overall level of support remains substantial. In 1987/8, the Government spent £2.5 billion on support for the agriculture and food sector. Two-thirds of this was market support under the Common Agricultural Policy, the remainder being made up of national measures and assistance to farming in special areas.

All this assistance from the state has, however, been provided without any real reduction in the farmer's autonomy in making decisions about the way in which his or her farm is run. The state has extended through the farm gate, but it has done so in a benevolent way which has not undermined the commercial freedom of the farmer. Indeed, there is a dual autonomy: '*first* the autonomy of the Ministry and of the farming community in the administration and implementation of agricultural policy; and *second* the autonomy of the farmer in making production and land use decisions' (Cox *et al.* 1986b, p. 186).

The nature of the relationship between state and farmer is well illustrated by a pamphlet issued by MAFF in 1984. It explained to farmers how they could obtain grants under approved development plans, a scheme putting into effect a 1979 EC directive on farm modernisation. The maximum grant per business was just over £136,000. The pamphlet explained that ADAS could be asked to draw up the development plan. A fee would be charged for this service, but a grant could be claimed on this fee. Farmers would also be required to keep accounts to show how they had spent the money, but a grant was available to help them keep the necessary records.

## The sources of effective influence

How are we to explain the exercise of effective influence by farming organisations for much of the post-war period? As pointed out in the last chapter, farmers were much less influential in the 1930s. 'In the 1930s it was industry and the Dominions which were dominant interests in agricultural policy and this resulted in an agricultural policy which favoured consumers over farmers' (Smith 1988, pp. 5−6). The Cabinet ruled out action to help British agriculture on several occasions 'on the grounds it would harm the Dominions' (p. 7).

The situation was changed by the post-war settlement in agriculture embodied in the 1947 Agriculture Act, although this settlement had already been presaged by changes taking place in the relationship during wartime. The 1947 Act created the context in which post-war agricultural policy was developed. It was a government initiative intended to secure a range of objectives such as a reliable, domestically produced supply of cheap food and adequate earnings for farmers and farm workers. One of its motivations was to prevent a repetition of the slump that had followed the First World War, and the subsequent inter-war depression in agriculture. The basic philosophy was an expansionist one, with the objective of reducing Britain's dependence on imports of temperate foodstuffs (an objective that was largely achieved). The opportunity for increased NFU influence thus arose from changes in government policy. In particular, the 1947 Act created a legal obligation on MAFF 'to consult with such persons as appear to represent the interest of the producer', which in practice meant the NFU. The main new mechanism introduced by the Act was the setting of guaranteed prices through an annual price review by MAFF in consultation with the NFU. This annual review has, of course, been supplanted by negotiations in Brussels since Britain joined the EC.

The agricultural policy community remains a relatively closed one which pivots around the relationship between MAFF and the NFU, although the Country Landowners Association (CLA) also plays a significant role. The close partnership between the two organisations has flourished since the 1947 Act. This does not mean, of course, that the two partners never disagree, and the strains have intensified in the 1970s and 1980s. Nevertheless, the relationship has been based on a shared perception of the desirability of a strong British agriculture, 'strong' being interpreted, until the recent past, as the maximisation of production, and the substitution of capital for labour inputs.

One sign of the underlying strength of the relationship is to be found in the movement of staff between the Ministry and the pressure group. For example, in 1979 MAFF's second permanent secretary until 1978 became the NFU's policy adviser on European affairs, and in 1981 an under-secretary became the NFU's chief economic and policy adviser (Doig 1986, p. 41). MAFF's significance to the farming lobby can be judged by the fact that a major proposal of reformers has been to convert it from a client-oriented ministry into a more broadly based Department of Rural Affairs which would have a general responsibility for the rural economy and the rural environment. Another suggestion has been that its food and health responsibilities should be transferred to the Department of Health, or a new consumer affairs ministry, while responsibility for farming is moved to the Department of Trade and Industry. Options of this kind were being openly supported by Conservative backbenchers early in 1989. If any of these changes were to take place, they would represent a real weakening of the strength of the farming lobby.

The position of agriculture within government is further strengthened by the fact that there are no fewer than three ministries that have a responsibility for agriculture: MAFF, the Scottish Office and the Northern Ireland Office (the Welsh Office also has some agricultural responsibilities). This means that on many interdepartmental committees there are three representatives looking at matters from the agricultural viewpoint. To complete the symmetry of the partnership, there are separate farmers' unions for Scotland and Northern Ireland.

Countervailing institutional interests within government are relatively weak, or take relatively little interest in agricultural matters. In the immediate post-war period there was a distinct Ministry of Food which took a consumerist stance, but this was eventually merged (or, indeed, submerged) in MAFF. Officials in the Ministry of Food correctly anticipated that a merged ministry:

> would be subjected to heavy pressure from the National Farmers' Union at Ministerial level (and) it would rapidly degenerate into the kind of department that the Ministry of Agriculture is today, i.e. primarily concerned with looking after the farmers' interest.
>
> (MAF 127/269, quoted in Smith 1988, p. 16)

From 1974 to 1979 there was a Department of Prices and Consumer Protection represented by its minister at Cabinet level, and one of the holders of the job, Shirley Williams, placed particular emphasis on defending the interests of consumers in relation to the agricultural lobby. In general, however, agricultural policy has been developed in the absence of much in the way of effective intervention from elsewhere in government, in particular from the Treasury and the Cabinet. Treasury influence was limited by the conventions of the price review, and by the fact that it confined itself to a general evaluation of policies rather than more detailed technical analysis (Self and Storing 1962, p. 78). As far as the Cabinet is concerned, it has often been prepared to make 'substantial last-minute concessions sooner than face an open disagreement with the [National Farmers'] union' (p. 79).

The Crossman diaries show all too clearly that Cabinet ministers often did not fully understand the implications of the decisions they were making about agricultural policy. Crossman, as a farm owner, knew all too well that his colleagues were giving farmers a good deal when they thought they were being tough. On one occasion, Cabinet assented to a compromise which in fact represented 'a very generous concession to the farming industry' (Crossman 1976, p. 239). On another occasion, Crossman gave the NFU leadership a private briefing on the farm price review, advising them that 'if they wanted to exert pressure the best thing to do was to require very little that would be a burden on public expenditure because the Treasury would much prefer to help the farmers at the expense of the housewife and the cost of living' (1977, p. 839).

The outsider wishing to engage in debate about agricultural policy faces two layers of complexity which, it can be argued, are deliberately enhanced to keep the policy community closed. On the one hand, there is a body of technical information concerned with the practice of farming: for example, information about the sowing, protection against disease, and harvesting of crops. On the other hand, there is the sometimes unbelievable complexity of the systems of agricultural support: for example, the operation of the 'green currency' system in the European community, or the intricacies of the milk marketing scheme in Britain. Very often, the only way of learning about these matters is from the agricultural policy community, which reacts to outsiders either by trying to co-opt them, or by trying to shut them out (I have experienced both stratagems in my research on agriculture).

## The strength of the NFU

Graham Wilson (1978, p. 31) has noted that 'In spite of the fact that Great Britian has long been one of the world's most urbanized countries, its National Farmers' Union is arguably the best and organizationally strongest of western agricultural interest groups.' Indeed, the fact that the basic political environment is potentially inhospitable requires strength and sophistication on the part of the leading farmers' organisation. The

National Farmers' Union is a very well-resourced organisation. Lowe *et al.* (1986) report the staff level of the NFU as being around 840, more than twice the number of persons employed by the CBI. Admittedly, two-thirds of these employees are located away from London, and are mainly engaged in providing services to members, principally selling insurance. Even so, the NFU clearly does not lack basic organisational resources.

The NFU has also been successful in organising the vast majority of farmers, and in managing potential internal conflicts. The leadership of the union is often drawn from arable farmers from eastern and central England who are able to spare the time to attend meetings in London (although the president at the time of writing comes from a different background). However, through its commodity committees, and the involvement of the county branches in the decision-making process, care is taken to ensure that, for example, the concerns of dairy farmers in the west of the country are not neglected. One particular rule ensures that the NFU's president retains broadly based support among the membership. He or she is re-elected annually, and has to have 80 per cent support to remain in office. In other words, dissatisfaction among 21 per cent of the activists is sufficient to eject the president from office.

The NFU has also been very sophisticated in its adjustment to changing circumstances. It has not clung to existing policies when it is apparent that they no longer command political support. Cox *et al.* (1988) show how the union shifted from its initial opposition to dairy quotas to support for quotas on cereals as a palatable alternative to price cuts. Similarly, the NFU has been able to accommodate pressure for new environmental controls, although it is perhaps the CLA that has been 'remarkable for its preparedness to countenance a major re-think of the system of agricultural support to achieve rural policies of greater economic, environmental and political sustainability' (p. 334). It should be noted, however, that the CLA's proposals seek to preserve 'exceptionalism' by continuing to exclude planning controls over agricultural operations.

The NFU has generally been able to keep its members under control and to discourage them from engaging in militant actions which might antagonise public opinion. One NFU official commented in interview:

> We are in a difficult position in that the British public are more sensitive to clean tactics and dirty tactics in promoting an issue. We can use publicity measures, but we can't use militant action, particularly demonstrations that get violent, tractors blocking up towns — we tend to steer clear of that.

Nevertheless, farmers have resorted to demonstrations from time to time. Crossman records a series of such incidents, noting that 'Those of us in the Cabinet who want to give the farmers something realise that they are trying to force our hands and that whatever we do, they won't be grateful, so this time we will probably be really tough' (1977, p. 798). Some of the most serious demonstrations took place in 1974 when 'flying pickets' of farmers massed at Holyhead and other ports to prevent the unloading of Irish beef.

In terms of 'insider' politics, the NFU has always made effective use of its membership of the CBI and the support it can draw from elsewhere in the industrial and financial community. In particular, support has been available from firms which make key inputs used by farmers, such as fertilisers, agrochemicals and agricultural machinery, and which therefore have a clear interest in the wellbeing of agriculture.

One potential explanation that cannot account for the strength of the farming lobby is the farm vote. There are no constituencies in Britain where those employed in agriculture even approach a majority of the voters, although perhaps one should take into account that persons employed in jobs servicing agriculture may also be concerned about the state of the industry. Even so, if the 'farm vote' has had an impact on MPs in the past, it has been through an exaggeration of its real impact. What is certainly the case is that farmers make up a higher percentage of MPs and peers than would be justified by their representation in the population at large.

## Forestry: a closed policy community

If the agricultural policy community is relatively closed, that of forestry comes close to being hermetically sealed. As one commentator has remarked, 'Forestry policy has been made "out of sight" and "out of mind"' (*Financial Times*, 27 April 1988). The forestry sector has received levels of financial assistance and, until recently, tax concessions that are difficult to justify in terms of its contribution to the national economy.

At the centre of the forestry policy community stands the Forestry Commission which combines the functions of being a forestry enterprise in its own right with regulating the private sector of forestry, which is exempt from normal planning controls. The private forestry sector has changed in the last two decades with the emergence of large forestry management companies. The four largest management companies account for the majority of new large-scale planting in Britain. The relations of these companies with the Forestry Commission 'are close, with movements of personnel between them' (Stewart 1987, p. 12).

The Forestry Commission was set up in 1919 in response to a strategic shortage of timber in the First World War. Not only was it the first state-owned production industry in Britain, but it has also escaped recent pressures for privatisation, apart from some disposals of land. Proposals to privatise forestry were produced by a think tank within the Environment Department in 1987, but were subsequently shelved, apparently after pressure from the forestry industry. Very few other sectors of the economy have been able to escape from the Government's privatisation programme.

Responsibility for forestry within government is shared between MAFF, the Welsh Office and the Scottish Office, although, given the importance of forestry in Scotland, it is the Scottish Office which acts as the 'lead' department. One consequence is that 'English MPs of all parties are reluctant to interfere in what appears to be a largely Scottish question' (p. 44). Nevertheless, it is clearly an area in which interdepartmental conflicts are an important consideration. For example, an announcement in the spring of 1988 by the Environment Secretary that large-scale upland conifer planting would be discouraged in England was not followed by similar announcements by the Scottish and Welsh offices.

The industry itself is well organised. One of the predecessor organisations of Timber Growers UK was formed with assistance not only from the CLA but also from the Forestry Commission (Lowe *et al.* 1986, p. 96). In 1987 the industry responded to growing political criticism by forming the Forestry Industry Committee of Great Britain, which encompasses all forest industry activities from silvicultural research to the commercial processing of timber. The Forestry Commission's network of advisory committees is 'dominated by the representatives of forest owners and wood-using industries, though they have now been expanded to include representatives of conservation and recreation interests and other land users' (Stewart 1987, p. 17).

The industry has received substantial support from the Treasury, particularly when viewed in relation to its size (43,000 employees). The Forestry Industry Committee of Great Britain has estimated tax allowances and Forestry Commission grants as £17−19 million each year for the private sector, and £53 million grant-in-aid to the Forestry

Commission. The Commission has been required to meet a target rate of return of 3 per cent on its assets, compared with a target of 5 per cent set for all other investments. Moreover, the asset base is revalued at the beginning of each five-year period. Given the time that it takes a forest to grow, 'this treatment effectively writes off sunk costs every five years' (*Financial Times*, 27 April 1988). It is also apparent that the bulk of new planting is not achieving the modest 3 per cent return rate.

The forestry industry has a number of responses to the criticisms made of it. It likes to point out that only 10 per cent of Britain's land area is devoted to forests compared with an EC average of 25 per cent, and that Britain still imports over 90 per cent of its timber requirements. However, the distribution of forest in different countries is partly a reflection of geographical conditions and, in any case, import substitution is not a sensible policy if it involves a diversion of resources which could be used more effectively elsewhere. The industry has pointed out that other industries receiving government subsidy have a poor performance, but two wrongs do not make a right. The industry also emphasises the contribution it makes to rural employment in remote areas, but 'There is growing reliance on gangs of migratory workers, who do not contribute to the income of any one district' (Stewart 1987, p. 37). Perhaps the industry's strongest card is the recovery and growth of the forest products industry in Britain with substantial investment from Scandinavia and Canada taking place: for example, a new plant is coming on stream at Irvine in Scotland in 1989. Such plants will need an assured supply of domestic timber, and it is significant that some paper and board companies are involved in the Forest Industry Committee of Great Britain.

## Pressures for policy change

The calm of the policy community has been disturbed on a number of occasions by outside investigations. In 1972 there was an Interdepartmental Cost−Benefit Study by the Treasury which found, in summary, that there was little economic justification for current afforestation policies. No policy changes followed. There were critical reports from the Public Accounts Committee in 1979/80 and 1983/4, neither of which led to any change in policy. In 1986 the National Audit Office carried out a new review of the Forestry Commission. The report was highly critical, and the forestry industry admitted in its own response that 'The implications are that the forestry industry in Great Britain is not worthy of continued subsidy and support, and that scarce public-sector resources would be better employed in higher yielding areas of the economy' (Firn-Crichton-Roberts Ltd 1987, p. 7).

The industry was vulnerable on the tax front, given that the Government was concerned to reduce overall levels of taxation. The situation verged on the absurd. 'The most striking statistic is that tax incentives and grants turn a near zero rate of return on afforestation (excluding pruchases and sale of land) for the speedy planter of a typical Scottish estate into a return of 30 per cent per annum net of tax and of inflation, equivalent, for an investor paying income tax at the top rate, to a gross rate of 75 per cent in real terms' (Stewart 1987, p. 42). In his 1988 Budget speech, the Chancellor declared that the present system of forestry tax reliefs could not be justified, and the time had come to bring it to an end. He did this by taking commercial woodlands out of the income tax system altogether. He noted that it was a measure of the absurdity of the then system that total exemption of commercial woodlands from tax would actually lead to increased tax revenues of £10 million a year!

The tax changes were a heavy blow for the industry, although the blow was softened by the announcement of a new system of planting grants, nearly treble the level of the old grants for large plantations of conifers. It is difficult to estimate what the long-run effect of these changes will be, although 'while tax exemption brought in very wealthy outside investors, the new planting grants will encourage local landowners not in the highest tax brackets to plant their own land using the grants, instead of selling out to commercial forestry companies' (Mitchison 1988, p. 21). Overall, 'it is hard to avoid the conclusion that a real opportunity to produce a more relevant and publicly acceptable forestry policy has been missed' (*Financial Times*, 25 March 1988). Certainly, one of the consequences of the tax regime changes was to defuse the public debate about forestry policy. 'The public argument over forestry policy has abated noticeably since the Budget announcement in March', and in particular there was little more consideration of 'whether it is actually appropriate and sensible for Britain to grow conifers to feed its timber plants rather than import the wood from possibly cheaper sources' (*Financial Times*, 6 September 1988).

## The impact of afforestation on the environment

Apart from the debate about the economic viability of the British forestry industry, there has also been an increasingly intense argument about its environmental impact. Much of the concern has been focused on the visual impact of monotonous plantings of Sitka spruce in upland areas. Afforestation has led to 'the entire character of whole districts [being] completely transformed, particularly in Scotland, where afforestation is now regarded by many people as the dominant issue in the countryside' (Stewart 1987, p. 21). Concern has also been expressed about the impact of afforestation on bird populations. Generally, afforestation has the effect of replacing small populations of rare birds with special requirements by common forest birds. There are also concerns about the impact on soil and water.

These concerns have centred on a major battle between conservation and afforestation interests over the future of the 'Flow' Country in Caithness and Sutherland. This is a very remote area, as near to a wilderness as can be found in the British Isles. It is a vast area of relatively low-lying moorland and peat bog. Since 1981 Fountain Forestry has been buying up land in the Flow Country and planting it with trees. By 1987 around 12 per cent of the Flow Country had been planted, with another 5 per cent destined for planting (*Financial Times*, 4 February 1987). The plantations themselves are owned in 50-hectare blocs by private investors including show business and sporting personalities.

Clearly, planting changes the appearance of this, for Britain, unique sub-Arctic tundra and bog terrain. Much of the concern, however, has been about the impact on the area's bird population, for which the Flows offer a diverse habitat. The Flow Country is the breeding ground of about 70 per cent of Britain's one thousand or so greenshanks (a wader), and the RSPB claims that 688 pairs of greenshanks have disappeared because of afforestation. The area is also home to one-third of the dunlin population, to golden plovers, merlins and other species.

The RSPB, with more than half a million members, is a formidable adversary, and the director of Fountain Forestry's Scottish operations has stated that 'this whole debate would have remained a low-key issue if the RSPB hadn't gotten [*sic*] involved' (*Atlantic*, November 1988, p. 39). There are also concerns that afforestation will disrupt the red deer population, the hunting of which is big business in the area. Trenches dug to drain the bog could leach debris into the rivers, polluting them and disrupting the fish population. Fishermen from around the world are willing to pay well to fish in the area for salmon and trout. The Nature Conservancy Council (NCC) takes the view that the area already lost to forestry 'represents perhaps the most massive single loss of important wildlife habitat since the Second World War' (*Atlantic*, November 1988, p. 40). Several thousand hectares have been designated as Sites of Special Scientific Interest by the NCC.

On the other side of the argument are Fountain Forestry, the Highland Regional Council, and the Highlands and Islands Development Board. Fountain Forestry employs two hundred workers in Caithness and all but forty of all these would have to be laid off if planting ceased. This is a large number in a remote area with few alternative employment opportunities. After all, some people want to make a living and raise families in the area in which they were born, and their claims have to be balanced against those of the greenshank (there are limits to the extent to which additional employment could be created in tourism).

The Secretary of State for Scotland appears to have attempted to find a compromise between the conflicting interests, safeguarding a substantial area of peat moor, including the most important bog systems and bird habitats, but allowing planting to continue on some sites. In 1988 he decided that forestry grants should be allowed in four of the seven cases on which he had to decide because of NCC objections. This did not please the NCC, who complained that the Scottish Office was applying a 'dripping tap' policy (*Independent*, 4 June 1988). The Scottish Office has argued that the additional planting is necessary to the local economy and to help reach the Government's target of 33,000 hectares of new forest a year. On the whole, the arguments of the producers appear to have prevailed over those of the conservationists.

As the forestry industry itself recognises, 'The financial support, numbers employed and votes at risk in the forestry industry are tiny' (*Forestry and British Timber*, April 1988). However, the relative insignificance of the industry has in some ways been an asset, as it has helped to keep the industry away from public attention. The concerns expressed by environmentalists have changed this to some extent, but the various critical reports on state support for the industry have had only limited impact. Policy continues to be made largely by the Forestry Commission and the Scottish Office in consultation with industry interests. The more general problem is that 'At present no institution is competent to seek an integrated view of the public interest for the countryside' (Stewart 1987, p. 50).

## Is the farming lobby losing ground?

The agricultural policy community has been described as 'increasingly beleaguered' (Cox *et al.* 1988, p. 326). Conversations with farmers certainly confirm the view that they see themselves as under siege from hostile political forces. Experienced politicians such as the chairman of the Conservative backbench agriculture committee have argued that 'The influence of the NFU is not as strong as it was' (*Independent*, 24 December 1988). In 1987 the president of the NFU was reported to have been told by the chairman of the Conservative backbench 1922 Committee, 'we cannot regard your organisation any longer as anything more than a mere trade association' (*Independent*, 24 December 1988).

There are a number of reasons why the farmers might be losing ground politically. First, the best political environment for farmers was probably during the 1950s and 1960s, with MAFF committed to expansion and the annual price review being conducted away from the glare of everyday politics. 'Until very recently, agricultural issues excited neither much public nor political interest' (*Financial Times*, 25 January 1989). Since Britain joined the European Community, agricultural issues have become more politicised. The EC spends more on the CAP than any other aspect of its activities, and voters have become aware of the size and cost of farm supluses.

Disputes over the level of the 'green pound' during the 1974−9 Labour Government probably did more than anything else to propel agricultural issues to the centre of the political stage. The green currency systems of the EC are a highly complex matter but, in broad outline, the pound used to calculate agricultural support prices has a different value from the pound used for other transactions. (For a fuller account, see Grant 1981). The Labour Government kept the green pound overvalued as a means of holding down the price the consumer pays for his or her food. The issue became increasingly politicised, culminating in a defeat for the Government on a Conservative motion on the subject in 1978. (A bizarre aspect of the whole affair was complaints by an Ulster Unionist that the term 'green pound' was offensive because of its Republican connotations.) The broader significance of the green pound controversy was that it represented a breakdown of the bipartisan consensus on agricultural policy issues which had generally served the farmers well.

The election of the Thatcher Government in 1979 also posed new problems for the farming lobby. As one Conservative MP has commented:

> The Thatcher years have been anti-coporatist years and we have seen a diminution of all interest groups. The farming lobby is the greatest Conservative interest group, but it has not been immune from that process.
> (*Independent*, 24 December 1988)

Thatcherism is, after all, opposed to subsidisation of industry, so why should agriculture be treated any differently? There is a theoretical case for intervention, based on the findings of agricultural economics about the difficulty of attaining an equilibrium position between supply and demand in relation to agriculture commodities. However, the market stabilisation arrangements that are required to cope with these problems are less extensive and expensive than current levels of intervention. Conservative backbenchers have shown increasing concern about the failure to apply free-market principles to agriculture, and the waste inherent in existing arrangements: for example, note the critical publications of Sir Richard Body MP.

The composition of the Conservative membership of the Commons has changed, with fewer 'knights from the shires' and more urban MPs sitting for rural areas. Attendance at the Conservative backbench agriculture committee is said to have dropped from around one hundred a week to ten or twenty. One Oxfordshire MP is reported as commenting, 'I tell my farmers they represent 3 per cent of the electorate. But I've got 5 per cent who are Bangladeshis' (*Independent*, 16 December 1988). Traditional landowning interests are, admittedly, more strongly represented in the House of Lords.

In 1987 the Prime Minister reprimanded the NFU after they had, probably unwisely, passed a vote of no confidence in her Government's agricultural policy and had called for the resignation of the Minister of Agriculture (he was defended at the time by the Prime Minister, but was subsequently dismissed). In a strongly worded letter to the president of the NFU, Mrs Thatcher commented:

> You are ready to acknowledge the problems of over-production. But you seem unwilling to face up to the consequences of tackling them.
>
> (*Financial Times*, 14 February 1987)

The Prime Minister is a skilled interpreter of the popular political mood, and there is no doubt that her remarks reflected a shift in public opinion about farmers. Britain has been an urbanised country since the nineteenth century, but it is only with mass ownership of the motor car that the countryside has come to be used regularly by the urban population as a recreational amenity. They do not always like what they see, for example hedges and copses removed by arable farmers to create 'prairie' farming conditions which are visually unattractive and provide an unfavourable habitat for birds and other wildlife. These concerns about the physical appearance of the countryside are reinforced by other worries about the use of pesticides and fertilisers, and about the conditions in which animals, particularly poultry, are kept.

Farmers have benefited from being seen as trustees of the countryside.

nurturing it to be handed on to the next generation. The urban majority of the population are no longer sure that they fulfil that role. The tension between more tradition and more business-oriented farmers is well captured in the popular radio series, *The Archers*, which has a large urban audience. Philip Archer inherited Brookfield from his father and will no doubt in time pass it on to his son, David. Although Phil Archer runs his farm on businesslike lines, he is cautious about change, and has a sentimental streak. Brian Aldridge, who purchased another farm nearby, sees farming as a way of making money. With his Range Rover and car telephone, frequently dashing off to conferences on the business of farming, he represents another type of farmer, and one that the town dweller suspects is becoming all too common.

All these tensions are reflected in splits in the unity of the farming movement. It is difficult to sort out cause and effect here: have farmers become more disunited because they are operating in a more difficult political environment, or has their disunity undermined their influence? Probably both factors are at work. What is clear is that 'The internal consensus, so essential to a working partnership with the state and achieved relatively easily in the days when mixed farming predominated, is currently in some disarray' (Lowe *et al.* 1986, p. 91). In particular, tensions between 'corn and horn' (arable farmers and livestock producers) have come to the surface. Breakaway organisations have been formed for tenant farmers and small farmers.

## Agriculture and the environment

Is the farming lobby really losing significant ground, or has it adapted relatively effectively to a changing political environment? This issue can usefully be considered in relation to the growing environmental concern about a number of farming activities. For example, there has been growing concern about high nitrate levels in water, particularly in eastern England. Current high nitrate levels may be caused as much by the ploughing up of meadow in the Second World War as by the encouragement given to farmers in the post-war period to use more nitrate fertilisers. In any event, EC limits for nitrate levels in water are being exceeded in some areas, and there is concern about a possible link between high nitrate consumption and stomach cancer. There may have to be water protection zones in which the use of nitrate fertilisers is limited or banned.

The impact of growing environmental concern on the agricultural policy community has been monitored over a number of years in a series of publications by Graham Cox, Philip Lowe and Michael Winter. One of their concerns has been to study the way in which particular problems have been approached and dealt with through the political process. It will not be possible to discuss specific issues here; rather the emphasis will be on the general lessons about the nature of the political process that emerge from their work.

First, it is clear that MAFF has been impervious to environmental pressures. Environmentalists have found MAFF the 'least accessible government department and the most unreceptive one' (Cox et al. 1985, p. 147). The policy community has remained closed to environmental interests, who have not been given consultative status. MAFF has responded to changes in public opinion 'with a combination of apparent disregard and studied gradualism, consistently [working] to affirm the existing order, defending meanwhile its distinctive administrative territory' (1986b, p. 193). In particular, 'the farming lobby has sought strenuously to maintain the integrity of the agricultural policy community by expanding the range of issues covered by established corporatist arrangements' (1988, p. 336). The Farming and Wildlife Advisory Group (FWAG) has operated 'as an informal and conservation-minded version of ADAS' (1986b, p. 199). The more conservative environmental groups belong to FWAG (the CPRE rather than Friends of the Earth), environmental issues are narrowed down to those of wildlife habitat and landscape quality, and in these ways the political issues are confined to the middle ground.

Does the emerging environmental policy community counterbalance that of agriculture? Not really. 'Most groups enjoy reasonable access to the DoE., but the Department does not play a role for environmental interests equivalent to that played by MAFF which promotes agricultural interests' (Cox and Lowe 1983, p. 270). The two policy communities differ in a way which is generally beneficial to farming interests. 'The policy community for rural conservation is characterised as large, diverse and pluralistic; that for agriculture as small, tightly-knit and corporatist' (Cox et al. 1986a, p. 16).

The farming lobby has had to give some ground to the environmentalists. The Halvergate marshes are important to conservationists as the last large area of open grazing marsh in eastern England. Lowe et al. (1986, p. 300) regard it as 'the principal case in landscape protection politics'. Farmers in the area wanted to drain the marshes and convert them into arable land. What ensued was a political struggle between a 'conservation camp' linked to the Department of the Environment, and a well-organised 'drainage camp' linked to MAFF. Friends of the Earth were actively involved, peacefully occupying farms where drainage work was started. The political crisis became so serious that the Prime Minister had to intervene personally, settling the argument in favour of the Department of the Environment (p. 296). A conservation scheme was drawn up which funded compensatory payments to farmers maintaining traditional grazing practices.

What this example illustrates is the general point that the farming lobby has been able to ensure that a particular view of environmental protection, based on compensation for property rights, has predominated. Having accepted production controls, it is difficult for farmers to argue against the principle of environmental controls. If they can secure payment for maintaining the countryside in a particular way, such controls may even benefit them. After all, 'In a context where land values are falling and the search for alternative sources of farm income is increasingly pressing, owning land which carries a designation may come to be seen as advantageous rather than, as formerly, entailing a penalty' (Cox et al. 1988, p. 324).

The influence of the farming lobby has been eroded in recent years, while environmental organisations have grown in terms of membership support and staff resources (as was shown in Tables 1.1 and 1.2). Even so, farmers' organisations remain among the more effective pressure groups. A really significant setback would be the abolition of MAFF in its present form, and substantial reductions in the level of subsidy paid to farmers. Mrs Thatcher would probably have liked to introduce more of a free market in agriculture, but a major constraint she faces is that the European Community has a major influence on agricultural policy, and is mindful of the needs of the larger farming populations of other European countries.

There is, however, scope for national action, and the Agriculture Minister at the time of writing, John MacGregor, a former Treasury minister, cancelled several grant schemes in 1988 that had been available for years to farmers to improve their productivity. These included grants for new roads in farmland, and for new field-drainage schemes which permitted the conversion of pasture to cereal-producing land. Such grants were replaced by grants with environmental rather than production objectives. Grants to reduce farm pollution incidents by promoting safer silage and slurry handling are to be increased to £50 million in the period up to 1991, while grant aid has been introduced to regenerate derelict farm woodlands, and to repair traditional farm buildings.

One of the difficulties of developing a more satisfactory agricultural policy is that the preferences of the population at large often appear to be somewhat confused. For example, they want subsidies to be reduced or even eliminated, but they do not want a landscape littered with abandoned farms and overgrown fields; they want stricter environmental controls, but they want food supplies to be reasonably priced.

Public interest in agricultural policy has increased, but not to the extent that the debate has been prised away from the relatively closed agricultural policy community. A wider debate might eventually lead to the setting of new priorities, and the construction of a new agricultural settlement to replace that of the immediate post-war period. Such a settlement might satisfy the public's environmental concerns, and also give the industry a new stability within which it could plan for the future. To be effective, the new settlement would have to be constructed at the EC level, and the chances of achieving it there, given national policy differences, are even less than at the domestic level.

# 8

# Conclusions: Pressure Groups and Democracy

This concluding chapter will not attempt to summarise all the arguments reviewed in the book, but will concentrate on the implications of the discussion for the democratic process. In what ways do pressure groups contribute to, or detract from, democracy? There is a sense, of course, in which some of the really important questions about democracy in Britain in the 1980s and 1990s concern the emergence of a dominant-party system. Patrick Dunleavy (1988, p. 13) has provided an interesting explanation of what he understands by the emergence of such a system in Britain and its consequences:

> In these systems (such as postwar Japan, Sweden since the 1930s, or even France under de Gaulle) there is still genuine and even intense electoral competition. But a single party commands so large and so assured a share of the vote that it is permanently in government and can realistically never be beaten. The dominant party monopolises control of state power, and its influence progressively extends through virtually all other organs of the state (such as local government or supposedly independent institutions). Its ideology suffuses the political system and sets the terms of debate.

## Thatcherism and pressure group activity

In such a situation, effective, sustained opposition is difficult, although it may be that campaigning pressure groups have something to contribute in that area. Before tackling more general issues about pressure groups and democracy, it is necessary to review the implications of Thatcherism for group activity. It is relatively easy to trace a number of short-run impacts that Thatcherism has had on pressure group activity, such as the downgrading of tripartite arrangements compared with the 1970s. What is more difficult to assess is the long-run consequences of the Thatcher Government for pressure groups.

One of the reasons is that, at the time of writing, one of the most significant future events in British politics is unknown: the manner and timing of Mrs Thatcher's departure. It is a measure of her impact on British politics that this should be a highly significant event in a way in which previous prime ministerial departures have not been. It does matter whether Mrs Thatcher leaves office early in the 1990s or at the turn of the century (although somewhere in the middle of the 1990s is perhaps the most likely departure date). It also matters whether she has to leave office because of electoral defeat (or such a large reduction in her majority that it stimulates party restiveness about her position), or whether she leaves office at a time of her own choice.

These factors aside, it is difficult to be certain about the ideological legacy of Thatcherism. Indeed, it is open to question whether Thatcherism is really an ideology, or simply a mixture of some strongly held convictions combined with an ability to be tactically flexible when putting the principles into practice. A parallel is often made with de Gaulle and Gaullism, not least because both Mrs Thatcher and de Gaulle were nationalists who sought to enhance their country's standing in the world. However, Gaullism disappeared as an 'ideology' once de Gaulle left political life. His lasting legacy was the political institutions of the Fifth Republic, which have continued to serve France well.

Mrs Thatcher has made an important impact on British political life in such areas as privatisation and the reduction of trade union power. Her main political legacy may appear to be the creation of a dominant-party system with the Conservatives as the party of government, although she has been greatly assisted in that task by the divisions and frequent ineffectiveness of the opposition. Indeed, she has not really succeeded in her longer-term political project of restructuring the party system so that it would be based on parties sharing similar values, excluding socialism, rather like the party system of the United States. (Her views on the creation of a two-party system in which socialism would be unacceptable are set out in her *Financial Times* interview of 14 November 1985; in her interview of 19 November 1986 she forecast that it would take perhaps two more terms of Conservative government to get rid of socialism as a second force in British politics.)

Mrs Thatcher has held equally strong views on the role of pressure groups in political life. In an interview on *Weekend World* on 15 January 1984 she stated, 'I can give you a check list now of the way in which we have tackled vested interest.' Certainly, the Government has dismantled tripartite arrangements, abolishing the Manpower Services Commission and downgrading the National Economic Development Council. A significant symbolic decision was taken in January 1989 when the leader of the electricians' union, expelled from the TUC, was given a place on the NEDC where the unions' representatives had always previously been drawn from the TUC. The representational dominance of the CBI on the employers' side was simultaneously undermined by the appointment of a representative of the chambers of commerce.

Even so, the traditional consultations between departments and pressure groups continue much as they have done throughout the post-war period. The biggest recent change has perhaps come from EC legislation, and the extent to which pressure groups are involved in detailed discussions about its implementation. Sectional groups have not had their traditional relationships disrupted very much, and cause groups have been offered new opportunities by, for example, Mrs Thatcher's professed enthusiasm for environmental policy.

Talk of a neo-liberal state form may, however, be premature; indeed, as Cox admits, 'the fully neo-liberal state may not be with us yet' (Cox 1988b, p. 232). Uncertainty about the future springs not so much from the question of what the Labour Party might do if it did come into office again (it still seems to have some kind of commitment to tripartism, if only for the lack of an alternative), but the more interesting problem of what the post-Thatcherite Conservative Party might be like. Will neo-liberals remain in control, will the 'one nation' Tories stage a comeback, or will there be some kind of post-Thatcherite synthesis? The third outcome is the most likely, but it still leaves open the question of what the content of the synthesis might be. The question of Mrs Thatcher's succession is a question about programme content and policy style, as much as about personalities. The Conservative Party in the twenty-first century will certainly be affected by the Thatcherite legacy, as will the whole of British politics, but the party may strike off in a new direction, perhaps under the leadership of one of the young 'high Tories' at present holding junior offices under Mrs Thatcher.

One of the younger 'high Tories' spoken of as a possible future leader of the Conservative Party is William Waldegrave. He seems to be unsympathetic both to corporatism of the kind which has been advocated by older 'one nation' Tories such as Sir Ian Gilmour and to the newer campaigning pressure groups. Waldegrave (1978, p. 122) regards corporatism as 'a pathology of Conservatism. Indeed, men of the utmost good-will in the Conservative tradition have veered too near it on occasion.' Although he rules out atomistic individualism, and praises the value of community, he rules out any notion of a Parliament of Interests, an idea later explicitly endorsed by Gilmour (1983, pp. 208–13).

As far as the newer campaigning groups are concerned, Waldegrave sees the trade unions, Shelter and the CPAG with the BMA, the arts lobby and the aircraft industry as 'skilful media manipulators' (Waldegrave 1978, p. 12) with the common objective of government action and expenditure. He sees the House of Commons as more 'interested in the scandal of the individual case or category of need, than in warning of the dangers which might ensue from meeting it' (pp. 12–13). The experience of the 1970s seems to have embedded within the Conservative Party a distaste for group-led pluralistic stagnation, although the practical consequences of such an orientation may be offset by the governmental habit of consultation.

## The case for pressure groups reviewed

Des Wilson, the well-known campaigner, has provided a list of key justifications for the existence of community/cause pressure groups. Of course, the population of pressure groups is also made up of sectional groups. Wilson has no time for 'vested interests, whose cause is usually maintenance of the status quo . . . irrespective of the implications for the community' (Wilson 1984, p. 2). Such groups are seen by him as part of a pattern of failure 'by our institutions, failures rooted in a deep bias towards the status quo, and vested interest in power and wealth'. It is in these and other failures 'that we find the outstanding argument for pressure groups' (p. 20). I am less sympathetic to the notion of 'cause groups good, sectional groups bad' which underpins much argument about pressure groups and the democratic process, a stance which ultimately reduces to a slightly more sophisticated way of saying one likes those pressure groups whose values one shares. Idealists, and those seeking to promote change, like Wilson, have a right to organise and be heard, but so do realists seeking to defend existing arrangements.

Wilson outlines seven key justifications for the existence of pressure groups, and the first three of these provide a good basis for reviewing many of the arguments about the contribution of pressure groups to democracy. (The last four are less convincing and will be considered more briefly.) The first is the argument that 'There is more to democracy than the occasional vote' (p. 21). Wilson is an enthusiast for participatory democracy, and he regards pressure groups as one way in which participation could take place. The counter argument for representative democracy is that many people consider that there are more meaningful or enjoyable activities in life than politics, and are therefore prepared to have persons sharing their general political outlook acting on their behalf.

Wilson deals with the argument that opposition parties provide a means whereby people can exercise their democratic rights by maintaining that they 'are themselves part of the governing system . . . Often specialist pressure groups are more effective than all-issue political parties in opposing "the system"'' (p. 21). What is clear is that the membership of cause groups has increased as the membership of political parties has declined. Many people are active in both political parties and cause groups, but it would seem that political parties have often seemed too unwelcoming, bureaucratic and preoccupied with questions of dogma to younger activists with a desire to bring about changes in society. Debates about state financing of political parties overlook the fact that political parties have suffered from a narrowing membership base.

Wilson claims that pressure groups counterbalance two inherent weaknesses in democracy, the first being that democracy 'does *not* work for all people' and that 'Pressure groups offer a chance for minorities and disadvantaged groups to argue their case' (p. 22). The second inherent weakness identified by Wilson is that electioneering encourages a short-term perspective on issues.

The first weakness identified by Wilson raises such fundamental issues about the relationship between pressure groups and democracy that a number of pages will have to be devoted to considering these problems before returning to Wilson's arguments. In particular, two counter arguments merit careful consideration. The first is that, in practice, it is easier to represent narrow, particular interests than more widely based, general interests. The second is that pressure group activity tends to reinforce existing biases within the political system rather than counteract them.

The idea that it is more difficult to organise general than particular interests recalls the discussion of Olson's theory of pressure groups in

Chapter 2. Some rather large potential interest groups do not seem to be very well organised. For example, pensioners have been represented by three organisations: Age Concern, Help the Aged, and the National Federation of Old Age Pensioners Associations (Whiteley and Winyard 1987, p. 20). Despite their efforts, the condition of the elderly poor has not improved significantly, and could be argued to be deteriorating. Retired persons seem to be less well organised than in the United States where the American Association of Retired Persons has 28 million members, making it the second largest political force after the Catholic Church. The gap in the British system has been spotted by a US-born businessman and former property developer who in 1988 launched a new Association of Retired Persons to represent the over-50s. This might seem to be a classic case of an entrepreneur-organiser mobilising an underrepresented group, although it remains to be seen how much success the new organisation will have. The real problem with representing the elderly is that they are not an undifferentiated category, but are divided on a number of lines, most notably between those pensioners who are entirely reliant on the state pension and any supplements they can obtain; those who have some savings they can draw on; and those who have, often quite substantial, private pensions in addition to the state pension. These three groups have very different needs and problems; it is difficult to unite them simply on grounds of age.

## The problem of consumer representation

A better example of a general interest is that of consumers. We are all consumers at one time or another, but producer interests are better organised. This is not accidental, but arises from 'the greater attention that the rational individual gives to his role as a producer compared with his role as a consumer' (Tivey 1974, p. 206). Consumers have not been well organised and they have tended to concentrate on consumer protection issues and the testing of products. Liberal economists would argue that the best protection available to the consumer is through the market mechanism, but this protects consumers only in the aggregate, and then only imperfectly, rather than as individuals. It could be argued that political parties should represent general interests such as consumers, and that they can be relied on to pass laws governing such questions as unsafe or unsatisfactory products. However, such issues are not generally very salient among voters, and governments have generally required some prodding to change the law. Bodies such as the Office of Fair Trading, and local authority trading standards offices, clearly have a role here in drawing attention to problems not adequately covered by existing legislation.

The inadequacy of consumer representation was reflected in the decision in 1975 to set up the National Consumer Council (NCC). The NCC is a rather unusual body in that it is funded by government through a grant-in-aid in order to lobby government on behalf of consumers. Given that consumer organisations have been predominantly middle class in membership, the NCC believes that it has 'a special obligation to speak up for the inarticulate and disadvantaged consumer' (1988 Annual Report, p. 17). Despite general guidelines of this kind, the problem remains of how the wishes of consumers are to be identified. The NCC does consult with consumer organisations through a National Consumer Congress, but most of the organisations have the kind of middle-class bias referred to earlier. A former chairman of the NCC, the late Michael Shanks, commented in the NCC's 1978 Annual Report (p. 5):

> [The consumer movement's] ability to identify and represent the views of consumers should be judged not in terms of any formalist vision of elective democracy, but by its capacity to reflect faithfully and energetically the preoccupations of consumers and to promote their interests.

It is certainly the case that the internal decision-making arrangements of many pressure groups would not meet conventional democratic tests, particularly in business associations where the different subscriptions paid by members are reflected to some extent in voting arrangements. Given its limited resources and a crowded agenda of potential issues, the NCC is perhaps best advised to get on with tackling the pressing issues facing it. It does make a serious effort to identify consumer concerns and needs through, for example, studies of the CAP or of air travel from a consumer viewpoint. The more general point that needs to be made is that government intervention to compensate for the poor organisation of general interests does bring certain problems in its train, not least how the interests at stake are to be identified and pursued.

## The reinforcement of existing biases?

Does pressure group activity tend to reinforce existing biases in the political system rather than counteract them? One concern about pressure groups, particularly the new campaigning pressure groups, is that they are overwhelmingly middle class in composition. It could be argued that this kind of middle-class political mobilisation reinforces existing biases in the political system in favour of the wealthier, better-educated section of the population (although it should be pointed out that it is only a minority of the middle class as a whole who are active in this way: the 'joiners', to use a sociological term which, perhaps unfortunately, has fallen out of favour).

It is important, however, to distinguish between the social composition of a pressure group and the objectives for which it is fighting. This is a point that has been made particularly by supporters of the environmental movement. Admittedly, 'the stereotype of the typical environmental activist as a university-educated middle class professional is pretty close to the truth' (Porritt and Winner 1988, p. 182). For example, 87 per cent of members of Friends of the Earth were found to be employed in senior managerial, administrative, professional, educational, technical or scientific occupations. However, Porritt and Winner go on to point out that Greens are concentrated in the 'caring' professions, and are usually committed to a 'non-materialist' life style. Such individuals do not fit in 'too neatly with the role assigned to them in the Marxist demonology as oppressors of the working class' (pp. 182–3). If there is one general criticism that may be made of environmentalists, it is perhaps that some of them are a little too ready to focus their criticisms on business and to ignore one of the most important, but very popular, sources of environmental damage, the motor car.

Even so, there are occasions when groups which claim to be concerned with protecting the environment may really be concerned with protecting the property values or living conditions of a particular group of relatively privileged individuals. Proposed locations for a third London airport attracted vigorous opposition from middle-class commuters, whose views tended to outweigh those of local working-class people who welcomed the employment opportunities that an airport would bring. There are occasions when pressure group activity may enable those who are economically successful to pull the ladder up behind them to the detriment of less well-placed groups. In general, however, one must not make the mistake of assuming an identity between a person's social class position and the views he or she holds.

A more serious difficulty arises from one of the general themes of this book: that most decisions of government are taken within relatively specialised policy communities, and that this tendency will be strengthened rather than weakened by the increased importance of the EC in the decision-making process. As was evident from the discussion in Chapter 7, policy communities differ in the extent to which they are open or closed to new entrants, but the more closed a policy community is, the more its decisions tend to be broadly beneficial to established interests. They may lose out on particular decisions, but in general they are able effectively to defend the status quo as a whole.

In well-organised policy communities, one tends to find some interests that are 'organised out' of the decision-making process, or that play a relatively limited role in it. One example is agricultural workers in the agricultural policy community. A study by Danziger of the political powerlessness of agricultural workers found that, in contrast to the employers, they lacked economic, political and social resources. 'Until now the history of the farmworkers' union has been one of outstanding powerlessness, interspersed with occasional successes and minor breakthroughs' (1988, p. 252). The cards often seemed to be stacked against the farm workers. For example, in its unsuccessful campaign to secure a ban on the weedkiller 2,4,5-T the agricultural workers' union faced 'the mobilisation of dominant social attitudes which associate scientific expertise with impartiality and correctness, often to the point of infallibility' (pp. 222–3).

It is not only relatively small, impoverished and isolated social groupings that lose out. General categories of the public at large also find themselves disadvantaged. Examples of this phenomenon can be found in policy communities where professional groups are able to deploy their expertise to develop a close relationship with government. Hence, the views of doctors tend to weigh very strongly in the health policy-making community compared with those of patients, although that is not to say that there may not sometimes be an identity of interest, as over the working hours of junior doctors. In matters relating to the operation of the legal system, the views of lawyers (strongly represented in Parliament) tend to weigh heavily with the government's law officers (themselves lawyers). Lord Mackay's proposals for a major reform of legal services might appear to be an exception to this rule. They certainly provoked considerable hostility from the legal profession. At the beginning of 1989, it was reported that, in the face of considerable opposition from peers, legislation on the proposals might have to be delayed.

## How can the balance between experts and citizens be redressed?

What can be done to redress the imbalance between expert pressure groups and the ordinary citizen? This is an area in which much depends on interventions by party politicians. For example, it has been argued that for many years the schools in Britain seemed to be run on the assumption that decisions were best taken by 'the experts' (teachers, local education authority officials, DES civil servants, and academic and other commentators). Relatively little regard was paid to the consumers, either to the parents as indirect consumers or, especially, to the views of the pupils themselves. Recent legislative changes have enhanced the role of parent governors in the running of schools, and some teachers have come to appreciate that there may be gains for them in a closer partnership with parents.

Another contemporary example of a minister attempting to challenge long-held assumptions and relationships is to be found in agriculture. The Minister of Agriculture in office in 1989, John MacGregor, has sought to reduce farm subsidies and to encourage farmers to supplement their income in other ways. If ministers are to be of any real value, they have to challenge existing assumptions held by policy communities, and introduce policies which bring about changes that benefit the public at large rather than a sectional interest. They should listen to what pressure groups have to say, and they should be prepared to modify their policies to remove real deficiencies that groups are able to identify, but they should not abandon their goals.

## The rest of Wilson's case

Having considered the fundamental issues raised by Wilson's first argument, it is now possible to return to his other arguments. As noted earlier, Wilson argues that a second inherent weakness in parliamentary democracy is that need to win elections leads to short-term political considerations prevailing over the longer-term interests of the country. I am less confident than he is that cause groups are able to take a long-term perspective. Too often they are ensnared in the assumptions of long-established policies, arguing for more resources to be devoted to such policies, or for improvements to be made in them, rather than for fundamental changes designed to meet long-term problems. In their concluding chapter, Whiteley and Winyard (1987) urge the poverty lobby to adopt a broader strategy which tackles economic issues of allocative efficiency. It is open to question, for example, whether social welfare organisations have considered the implications of an ageing population any more systematically than government.

Wilson's third main argument is that 'Pressure groups improve surveillance of government' (Wilson 1984, p. 23). Pressure groups can help to expose information which would otherwise remain secret. There have been important instances where pressure groups such as the CPAG have influenced public policy by leaking Cabinet documents. However, occasional exposures of this kind have to be set against a system of government which is permeated by a preoccupation with secrecy. Because the desirability of greater freedom of information has become a position shared by many academics and journalists commenting on British government, it is worth noting that there is a counterview which argues that open government would bring costs as well as benefits, particularly in relation to pressure group activity. Douglas Hurd, the Home Secretary at the time of writing, has commented that, if freedom of information 'simply means freedom for pressure groups to extract from the system only those pieces of information which buttress their own cause, then conceivably the result might be greater confusion and worse government' (*Royal Institute of Public Administration Report*, 1986, p. 1).

Wilson's other argument in favour of pressure groups as a means of improving surveillance of government is a more conventional one. He points out that they can bring to the attention of ministers and civil servants options and information of which they would not otherwise be aware. As was pointed out in relation to Whiteley and Winyard's work on the poverty lobby, this is an aspect of pressure group activity which is valued by government.

Wilson's other four arguments are less impressive. The argument that 'Pressure groups combat other pressure groups' (1984, p. 24), although particularly directed at redressing the influence of sectional groups, is really a reflection of conventional pluralist wisdom about countervailing groups. The argument that pressure groups persist in fighting for causes in which the media take only a short-term interest is a valid one, particularly in relation to the example Wilson gives of lead in petrol, but it is not a central argument in favour of pressure group activity. The argument that 'Community/cause groups offer people the weapons to fight on their own behalf' (p. 25) reflects Wilson's belief in the value of political participation, and the way in which group activity can build up the skills required for effective collective action. His final argument, that 'Pressure groups relieve frustration' (p. 25), is a double-edged one. No doubt they can act as a safety valve, and give people a sense of hope, but in doing so they may be serving more to promote political and social stability than to bring about real change.

Although I do not agree with many of his arguments, I agree with Wilson's general conclusion that 'pressure groups are not a threat to a genuine democracy, but a real contributor' (p. 25). I would insist that sectional groups have a contribution to make as well as cause groups. If the stake which 'vested interests' have is simply brushed aside, then serious damage may, quite unintentionally, be inflicted on the economy or on professions which make a worthwhile contribution to the community.

## The limits to pressure group power

If pressure groups were allowed to accumulate too much influence, then there would be a risk for democracy. That is why I have never been enthusiastic about a 'corporate state' (as distinct from more limited, consensus-building institutions such as the economic development committees run by the NEDC). As it is, pressure groups operate in a political system in which they are checked by other political forces. First, as has been pointed out a number of times, public opinion strongly influences the context in which pressure groups operate. The context in which environmental policy is made has changed because the public has become more concerned about environmental questions, and politicians of all parties have felt the need to make some response to this shifting climate of opinion. From the perspective of many environmentalists, the changes in public policy have been inadequate, but then environmental concerns have to be balanced against other considerations, particularly economic ones.

Pressure groups are also held in check by political parties, and by government ministers anxious to address a wider political audience than that of a sectional interest or cause group. Broadly based political parties have to appeal beyond the relatively narrow concerns of most pressure groups to win elections. Ministers wish to build their political and legislative reputations. Occasionally, an MP may build his or her reputation through the successful passage of a private member's bill (David Steel and abortion law reform is one example). In general, however, it is ministers who take important legislative initiatives. A minister whose career is built around publicity may ultimately suffer from the envy of his or her colleagues, but a minister who stays in his or her department, negotiating quietly with pressure groups, may win the gratitude of the relevant policy community, although not of the wider public.

Pressure group power is limited: it is based on the ability to persuade and to influence, rather than to take decisions or, with certain exceptions, to veto them. Groups which have enjoyed signifcant power at particular periods of time, such as the trade unions, have usually experienced a public reaction against them. Thatcherism in particular involves an autonomous political strategy developed by the leader of a political party who deliberately cuts across the wishes of established interests in an effort to establish a new political order.

One should not be too complacent about the position of pressure groups in the political system. The cards are often stacked in favour of established 'insider' groups. Policy communities are often too narrowly based, or too closed to new influences, producing policy solutions that represent incremental adjustments to existing policies — policies which are often based on a historical decision that is no longer relevant (such as the assumptions on which forestry policy was based after the First World War). Both inside and outside government, awkward questions need to be asked about existing policies. In this respect, the disappearance of the Central Policy Review Staff is to be regretted as it did offer a means of looking at long-term policy questions which could only be properly considered by transcending departmental boundaries and established policy communities.

Nevertheless, pressure groups do make a significant contribution to democracy, one which can be understood if we visualise a situation in which pressure groups were either banned or disregarded. Not only is the freedom to associate an important democratic principle, but pressure groups also offer an important mechanism through which the ruled can influence the rulers between elections. They also contribute to the quality of policy making by bringing the practical experience of, for example, business persons, health service administrators, or clients of the social services into what might otherwise be a rather insular debate in Whitehall about the development of policy. *Government* policy can only serve as *public* policy if it is based on consultations with an interested public.

Broader political principles are also at stake, beyond the desirability of having policies which are workable. At a time when many citizens are understandably disenchanted with political parties, involvement in pressure group activity has become increasingly attractive as an alternative means of influencing government. In a dominant-party system in which many intermediary institutions between the citizen and government have been dismantled (see Grant 1989), pressure groups have a greater importance as a source of constructive opposition to government policy, and as a means of ensuring that the distance between government and the governed does not become too great.

# References

Amery, L.S. (1947) *Thoughts on the Constitution*, Oxford University Press.
Atkinson, M.M. and Coleman, W.D. (1985) 'Corporatism and industrial policy', in A. Cawson (ed.) *Organized Interests and the State*, Sage.
Ball, A.R. and Millward, F. (1986) *Pressure Politics in Industrial Societies*, Macmillan.
Barnett, J. (1982) *Inside the Treasury*, André Deutsch.
Beer, S. (1956) 'Pressure groups and parties in Britain', *American Political Science Review*, vol. 50, no. 1, pp. 1–23.
Beer, S. (1965) *Modern British Politics*, Faber and Faber.
Beer, S. (1982) *Britain Against Itself*, Faber and Faber.
Boyle, E. (1971) Contribution to E. Boyle and A. Crosland in conversation with M. Kogan, *The Politics of Education*, Penguin.
Brickman, R., Jasanaoff, S. and Ilgen, T. (1985) *Controlling Chemicals: The Politics of Regulation in Europe and the United States*, Cornell University Press.
Brittan, S. (1964) *Steering the Economy*, Penguin.
Brittan, S. (1975) 'The economic contradictions of democracy', *British Journal of Political Science*, vol. 5, pp. 129–59.
Brittan, S. (1987a) 'The economic contradictions of democracy revisited', paper given to the Making of Economic Policy seminar, University of Warwick, to be published in *Political Quarterly* during 1989.
Brittan, S. (1987b) *The Role and Limits of Government*, Wildwood House, Aldershot.
Brittan, S. (1989) 'The Thatcher Government's economic policy', Esmee Fairbairn Lecture, University of Lancaster Economics Department.
Bruce-Gardyne, J. (1986) *Ministers and Mandarins*, Sidgwick and Jackson.
Brynin, M. (1988) 'False El Dorados', *New Statesman and Society*, 26 August 1988, pp. 28–9.

165

Buksti, J.A. and Johansen, L.N. (1979) 'Variations in organizational participation in government: the case of Denmark', *Scandinavian Political Studies*, vol. 2 (new series), no. 3, pp. 197–220.

Butt Philip, A. (1985) 'Pressure groups in the European Community', University Association of Contemporary European Studies Working Paper No. 2.

Byrd, P. (1988) 'CND: 30 years on', *Contemporary Record*, vol. 2, no. 1, pp. 10–12,

Cawson, A. (1986) *Corporatism and Political Theory*, Basil Blackwell.

Churchill, W.L. (1930) 'Parliamentary government and the economic problem', Romanes Lecture, Oxford.

Cm. 278 (1988) *DTI: The Department for Enterprise*, HMSO.

Coates, David (1972) *Teachers' Unions and Interest Group Politics*, Cambridge University Press.

Coates, Dudley (1984) 'Food law: Brussels, Whitehall and town hall', in D. Lewis and H. Wallace (eds) *Policies into Practice*, Heinemann.

Coffin, C. (1987) *Working with Whitehall*, Confederation of British Industry.

Coleman, W.D. (1987) 'Interest groups and democracy in Canada', *Canadian Public Administration*, vol. 30, no. 4, pp. 610–22.

Conroy, C. (1981) 'Public demonstrations: a Friends of the Earth view', paper presented at the Royal Institute of Public Administration conference on 'Public Influence and Public Policy'.

Cox. A. (1988a) 'Neo-corporatism versus the corporate state', in A. Cox and N. O'Sullivan (eds) *The Corporate State: Corporatism and the State Tradition in Western Europe*, Edward Elgar, Aldershot.

Cox, A. (1988b) 'The failure of corporatist state forms and policies in postwar Britain', in A. Cox and N. O'Sullivan (eds) *The Corporate State: Corporatism and the State Tradition in Western Europe*, Edward Elgar, Aldershot.

Cox, G. and Lowe, P. (1983) 'Countryside politics: goodbye to goodwill?', *Political Quarterly*, vol. 54, pp. 268–82.

Cox, G., Lowe, P. and Winter, M. (1985) 'Changing direction in agricultural policy: corporatist arrangements in production and conservation politics', *Sociologia Ruralis*, vol. 25, pp. 130–53.

Cox, G., Lowe, P. and Winter, M. (1986a) 'The state and the farmer: perspectives on agricultural policy', in G. Cox, P. Lowe and M. Winter (eds) *Agriculture: People and Policies*, Allen and Unwin.

Cox, G., Lowe, P. and Winter, M. (1986b) 'Agriculture and conservation in Britain: a policy community under siege', in G. Cox, P. Lowe and M. Winter (eds) *Agriculture: People and Policies*, Allen and Unwin.

Cox, G., Lowe, P. and Winter, M. (1988) 'Private rights and public responsibilities: the prospects for agricultural environmental controls', *Journal of Rural Studies*, vol. 4, pp. 323–37.

Crossman, R.H.S. (1976) *The Diaries of a Cabinet Minister: Volume 2*, Hamish Hamilton and Jonathan Cape.

Crossman, R.H.S. (1977) *The Diaries of a Cabinet Minister: Volume 3*, Hamish Hamilton and Jonathan Cape.

Danziger, R. (1988) *Political Powerlessness: Agricultural Workers in Post-War England*, Manchester University Press.

Davenport-Hines, R.P.T. (1984) *Dudley Docker: The Life and Times of a Trade Warrior*, Cambridge University Press.

Davies, M. (1985) *Politics of Pressure*, BBC Publications.

Devlin Commission (1972) *Report of the Commission of Inquiry into Industrial and Commercial Representation*, Association of British Chambers of Commerce/Confederation of British Industry.

Doig, A. (1986) 'Access to Parliament and the rise of the professional lobbyist', *Public Money*, vol. 5, no. 4, pp. 39—43.

Dowse, R.E. and Hughes, J. (1977) 'Sporadic interventionists', *Political Studies*, vol. 25, no. 1, pp. 84—92.

Dudley, G. (1983) 'The road lobby: a declining force?', in D. Marsh (ed.) *Pressure Politics*, Junction Books.

Dunleavy, P. (1988) 'Send her victorious', *New Statesman and Society*, 16 September 1988, pp. 12—15.

Eckstein, H. (1960) *Pressure Group Politics: The Case of the British Medical Association*, Allen and Unwin.

Edwards, R. (1988) 'Spirit of outrage', *New Statesman and Society*, 29 July 1988, pp. 16 and 18.

Elbaum, B. and Lazonick, W. (eds) (1986) *The Decline of the British Economy*, Clarendon Press.

Elliott, B., Bechhofer, F., McCrone, D. and Black, S. (1982) 'Bourgeois social movements in Britain: repertoires and responses', *Sociological Review*, vol. 30, no. 1, pp. 71—94.

Ennals, M. (1982) 'Amnesty International and human rights', in P. Willetts (ed.) *Pressure Groups in the Global System*, Frances Pinter.

Farago, P. (1987) 'Retail pressure and the collective reactions of the food processing industry', in W. Grant (ed.) *Business Interests, Organizational Development and Private Interest Government*, de Gruyter, Berlin.

Field, F. (1982) *Poverty and Politics*, Heinemann.

Finer, S.E. (1958) *Anonymous Empire*, Pall Mall.

Firn-Crichton-Roberts Ltd (1987) 'The forestry industry response to the National Audit Office report', Edinburgh.

Gilmour, I. (1978) *Inside Right*, Quartet.

Gilmour, I. (1983) *Britain Can Work*, Martin Robertson.

Grant, W. (1978) 'Insider groups, outsider groups and interest group strategies in Britain', University of Warwick Department of Politics Working Paper No. 19.

Grant, W. (1981) 'The politics of the green pound', *Journal of Common Market Studies*, vol. 19, no. 4, pp. 313—29.

Grant, W. (1983) 'Chambers of commerce in the UK system of business interest representation', University of Warwick Department of Politics Working Paper No. 32.

Grant, W. (1984) 'Large firms and public policy in Britain', *Journal of Public Policy*, vol. 4, pp. 1—17.

Grant, W. (1987) (with contribution by J. Sargent) *Business and Politics in Britain*, Macmillan.

Grant, W. (1989) 'The erosion of intermediary institutions', *Political Quarterly*, vol. 60, pp. 10–21.

Grant, W. and Marsh, D. (1977) *The CBI*, Hodder and Stoughton.

Grant, W., Nekkers, J. and van Waarden, F. (eds) (forthcoming) *Organizing Business for War*, Berg.

Grant, W., Paterson, W.E. and Whitston, C. (1988) *Government and the Chemical Industry*, Clarendon Press.

Grant, W. and Streeck, W. (1985) 'Large firms and the representation of business interests in the UK and West German construction industry', in A. Cawson (ed.) *Organized Interests and the State: Studies in Meso-Corporatism*, Sage.

Hall, P. (1986) *Governing the Economy*, Polity Press.

Heclo, H. and Wildavsky, A. (1974) *The Private Government of Public Money*, Macmillan.

Hindell, K. and Simms, M. (1974) 'How the abortion lobby worked', in R. Kimber and J.J. Richardson (eds) *Pressure Groups in Britain*, Dent.

Holbeche, B. (1986) 'Policy and influence: MAFF and the NFU', *Public Policy and Administration*, vol. 1, pp. 40–7.

Holmes, M. (1982) *Political Pressure and Economic Policy*, Butterworth.

Holmes, M. (1985) *The Labour Government 1974–79*, Macmillan.

House of Commons (1985) *First Report from the Select Committee on Members' Interests, 1984–85*, HMSO.

Isaac-Henry, K. (1984) 'Taking stock of the local authority associations', *Public Administration*, vol. 62, pp. 129–46.

Jordan, A.G. and Richardson, J. (1987) *Government and Pressure Groups in Britain*, Clarendon Press.

Kimber, R. and Richardson, J.J. (eds) (1974) *Pressure Groups in Britain*, Dent.

King, R. (1985) 'Corporatism and the local economy', in W. Grant (ed.) *The Political Economy of Corporatism*, Macmillan.

Kirchner, E. and Swaiger, K. (1981) *The Role of Interest Groups in the European Community*, Gower.

Kogan, M. (1975) *Educational Policy-Making*, Allen and Unwin.

Layfield Report (1976) Evidence of the National Association of Ratepayer Action Groups to the *Report on the Committee of Enquiry on Local Government Finance*, HMSO.

Lazonick, W. (1986) 'The cotton industry', in B. Elbaum and W. Lazonick (eds) *The Decline of the British Economy*, Clarendon Press.

Lively, J. (1975) *Democracy*, Basil Blackwell.

Lowe, P., Cox, G., MacEwen, M., O'Riordan, T. and Winter, M. (1986) *Countryside Conflicts: The Politics of Farming, Forestry and Conservation*, Gower.

Lowe, P. and Goyder, J. (1983) *Environmental Groups in Politics*, Allen and Unwin.

Lynn, L.H. and McKeown, T.J. (1988) *Organizing Business: Trade Associations in America and Japan*, American Enterprise Institute.

MacDougall, D. (1987) *Don and Mandarin: Memoirs of an Economist*, John Murray.

MAFF (1985) 'Review of food legislation: consultative document' (typescript), Ministry of Agriculture, Fisheries and Food.

MAFF (1987) *Survey of Consumer Attitudes to Food Additives*, HMSO.

Marsh, D. and Chambers, J. (1981) *Abortion Politics*, Junction Books.

Marsh, D. and Grant, W. (1977) 'Tripartism: reality or myth?', *Government and Opposition*, vol. 12, no. 2, pp. 194–211.

Marsh, D. and Read, M. (1988) *Private Members' Bills*, Cambridge University Press.

May, T. and Nugent, N. (1982), paper on thresholder groups presented at the annual conference of the Political Studies Association.

Medhurst, K. and Moyser, G. (1988) *Church and Politics in a Secular Age*, Clarendon Press.

Miller, C. (1987) *Lobbying Government*, Basil Blackwell.

Miller, C. (1988) (typescript) 'New lobbying techniques in Britain'.

Mitchell, N.J. (1987) 'Changing pressure-group politics: the case of the Trades Union Congress, 1976–84', *British Journal of Political Science*, vol. 17, pp. 509–17.

Mitchison, A. (1988) 'Carry on planting', *New Society*, 8 April 1988, pp. 21–2.

Moe, T.M. (1980) *The Organisation of Interests*, Chicago University Press.

Moran, M. (1983) 'Power, policy and the City of London', in R. King (ed.) *Capital and Politics*, Routledge and Kegan Paul.

Nettl, J.P. (1965) 'Consensus or élite domination: the case of business', *Political Studies*, vol. 8, pp. 22–44.

Newby, H., Bell, C., Rose, D. and Saunders, P. (1978) *Property, Paternalism and Power: Class and Control in Rural England*, Hutchinson.

Newton, K. (1976) *Second City Politics*, Oxford University Press.

Nugent, N. (1979) 'The National Association for Freedom', in R. King and N. Nugent (eds) *Respectable Rebels: Middle Class Campaigns in Britain in the 1970s*, Hodder and Stoughton.

Offe, C. (1981) 'The attribution of public status to interest groups: observations on the West German case', in S. Berger (ed.) *Organising Interests in Western Europe*, Cambridge University Press.

Offe, C. and Wiesenthal, H. (1985) 'Two logics of collective action' in C. Offe (principal author) *Disorganised Capitalism*, Polity Press.

Olson, M. (1965) *The Logic of Collective Action*, Harvard University Press.

Olson, M. (1982) *The Rise and Decline of Nations*, Yale University Press.

Oulès, F. (1966) *Economic Planning and Democracy*, Penguin Books.

Plowden, W. (1985) 'The culture of Whitehall', in D. Englefield (ed.) *Understanding the Civil Service*, Longman.

Porritt, J. and Winner, D. (1988) *The Coming of the Greens*, Fontana.

Presthus, R. (1964) *Men at the Top*, Oxford University Press.

Presthus, R. (1973) *Elite Accommodation in Canadian Politics*, Cambridge University Press.

Presthus, R. (1974) *Elites in the Policy Process*, Cambridge University Press.

Pross, A.P. (1986) *Group Politics and Public Policy*, Oxford University Press.

Public Policy Consultants (1987) 'The Government report', Public Policy Consultants, London.

Rhodes, R.A.W., Hardy, B. and Pudney, K. (1981) 'Public interest groups in central–local relations in England and Wales', *Public Administration Bulletin*, no. 36, pp. 17–36.

Richardson, J. (1977) 'The environmental issue and the public', in *Decision*

*Making in Britain: Block V*, Open University Press.

Richardson, J. and Jordan, G. (1979) *Governing Under Pressure*, Martin Robertson.

RIPA (1981) 'FOE's "street theatre" alerts public to issues', *RIPA Report*, no. 2, pp. 10–11.

Rose, R. (1974) *Politics in England Today*, Faber and Faber.

Ryan, M. (1978) *The Acceptable Pressure Group: A Case Study of the Howard League for Penal Reform and Radical Alternatives to Prison*, Saxon House, Farnborough.

Salisbury, R.H. (1984) 'Interest representation: the dominance of institutions', *American Political Science Review*, vol. 78, pp. 64–76.

Sargent, J. (1987) 'The organisation of business interests for European Community representation', in W. Grant, *Business and Politics in Britain*, Macmillan.

Scharpf, F. (1988) 'The joint-decision trap: lessons from German federalism and European integration', *Public Administration*, vol. 66, pp. 239–78.

Schattschneider, E.E. (1960) *The Semisovereign People*, Holt, Rinehart and Winston.

Schmitter, P.C. (1979) 'Still the century of corporatism?', in P.C. Schmitter and G. Lehmbruch (eds) *Trends Towards Corporatist Intermediation*, Sage.

Schmitter, P.C. (1985) 'Neo-corporatism and the state' in W. Grant (ed.) *The Political Economy of Corporatism*, Macmillan.

Schmitter, P.C. and Streeck, W. (1981) 'The organisation of business interests: a research design to study the associative action of business in the advance industrial societies of Western Europe', International Institute of Management labour market policy discussion paper.

Self, P. and Storing, H.J. (1962) *The State and the Farmer*, Allen and Unwin.

Smith, M.J. (1988) 'Consumers and British agricultural policy: a case of long-term exclusion', Essex Papers in Politics and Government No. 48, Department of Government, University of Essex.

Solesbury, W. (1976) 'The environmental agenda', *Public Administration*, vol. 54, pp. 379–97.

Stedward, G. (1987) 'Entry to the system: a case study of women's aid in Scotland', in A.G. Jordan and J. Richardson, *Government and Pressure Groups in Britain*, Clarendon Press.

Stewart, J.D. (1958) *British Pressure Groups*, Oxford University Press.

Stewart, M. (1984) 'Talking to local business: the involvement of chambers of commerce in local affairs', Working Paper No. 38, School for Advanced Urban Studies, University of Bristol.

Stewart, P.J. (1987) 'Growing against the grain: United Kingdom forestry policy 1987', a report commissioned by the Council for the Protection of Rural England.

Stocker, T. (1983) 'Pressures on policy formation' in J. Burns, J. McInerney and A. Swinbank (eds), *The Food Industry: Economics and Politics*, Heinemann.

Stocker, T. (1985) 'Nutrition: the food industry's role', *FDF Bulletin*, no. 1, pp. 8–16.

Stoker, G. (1988) *The Politics of Local Government*, Macmillan.

Streeck, W. (1983) 'Beyond pluralism and corporatism: German business associations and the state', *Journal of Public Policy*, vol. 3, pp. 265–84.

Stringer, J. and Richardson, J. (1982) 'Policy stability and policy change: industrial training 1964–82), *Public Administration Bulletin*, no. 39, pp. 22–39.

Taylor, E. (1979) *The House of Commons at Work*, 9th edn, Macmillan.

Theakston, K. (1987) *Junior Ministers in British Government*, Basil Blackwell.

Thomas, R.H. (1983) *The Politics of Hunting*, Gower.

Tivey, L. (1974) 'The politics of the consumer', in R. Kimber and J.J. Richardson (eds) *Pressure Groups in Britain*, Dent.

Truman, D. (1951) *The Governmental Process*, Knopf.

Turner, A. (1982) 'Food labelling', *FDIC Bulletin*, no. 21, pp. 21–7.

Waddington, J. (1985) 'Church and education', in G. Moyser (ed.) *Church and Politics Today*, T. and T. Clark, Edinburgh.

Waldegrave, W. (1978) *The Binding of Leviathan*, Hamish Hamilton.

Watkinson, Viscount (1976) *Blueprint for Survival*, Allen and Unwin.

Westergaard, J. and Resler, H. (1976) *Class in a Captialist Society*, Pelican.

Whiteley, P.F. and Winyard, S.J. (1987) *Pressure for the Poor*, Methuen.

Willis, D. and Grant, W. (1987) 'The United Kingdom: still a company state?', in M. van Schendelen and R. Jackson (eds) *The Politicisation of Business in Western Europe*, Croom Helm.

Wilson, D. (1984) *Pressure: The A to Z of Campaigning in Britain*, Heinemann.

Wilson, D. (1988) 'Inside local authorities', *Social Studies Review*, vol. 3, no. 4, pp. 135–9.

Wilson, G. (1978) 'Farmers' organizations in advanced societies', in H. Newby (ed.) *International Perspectives in Rural Sociology*, John Wiley.

# Index

abortion, 74–5, 84
agricultural interests, 6, 8–9, 17, 29, 133–51, *see also* National Farmers' Union
Agriculture, Fisheries and Food, Ministry of, 6, 57, 60, 64, 110, 136–7, 149, 150
Amery, L.S., 42, 165
Amnesty International, 13
animal rights groups, 18
Association of Petrochemical Producers in Europe, 100, 103
Atkinson, M., 37, 165

Ball, A.R., 43, 165
Barnett, J., 34, 165
Beer, S., 36, 165
Boyle, E., 79, 165
Brickman, R., 84, 165
British Medical Association, 2, 130, 155
Brittan, S., 36, 37–9, 41
bureaucracy, 44–6, 122, *see also* civil service
Bruce-Gardyne, J., 56, 62, 67–8, 69, 71, 72, 165
Buksti, J., 122, 166
business groups, 2, 22, 132, *see also* Confederation of British Industry
Butt Philip, A., 90, 95, 96, 97, 98–9, 104, 108, 111, 166

Byrd, P., 2, 114, 166

Campaign for Nuclear Disarmament, 2, 114
cause groups, 2, 5, 10, 12–14, 28, 48, 50, 55, 73, 80, 83, 114, 118, 119, 121–2, 154, 155, 156, 161
Cawson, A., 33, 166
CEFIC (European Council of Chemical Manufacturers' Federations), 100, 102, 103, 105–6
Centre for Policy Studies, 50
Chambers, J., 75, 79, 168
chambers of commerce, 86
charities, 11
Chemical Industries Association, 55, 64, 68, 80, 92, 97–8, 109
Child Poverty Action Group, 81, 82, 155
Church of England, 2, 10–11, 116
Churchill, W.L., 42, 166
City of London, 4, 120, 125, 130
civil service, 18, 19, 56, 57, 60–1, 83, 97, 105, 121, *see also* bureaucracy; government departments
Coates, David, 119, 166
Coates, Dudley, 61, 62, 65, 166
Coffin, C., 60, 166
Coleman, W., 37, 46, 165, 166

172

Commission of the EEC, *see* European
  Commission
Committee of Permanent
  Representatives, 95
Confederation of British Industry
  (CBI), 1, 16, 26, 34, 35, 42, 64,
  68, 70–1, 77, 80, 85, 108, 115,
  121, 124, 154
Conservative Government, 1970–4,
  35, 128
Conservative Government, 1979–,
  34–5, 38, 128, 130, 146–7
Conservative Party, 8, 77–8, 154
Conroy, C., 19, 166
consumers, 23, 43, 157–8
corporatism, 23, 24–5, 32–6, 39, 43,
  92, 112, 155
Council for the Protection of Rural
  England (CPRE), 13, 14, 80
Council of Ministers (of the European
  Community), 94–6, 104, 107–8
courts, 84–5
Cox, A., 25, 32, 35, 154, 166
Cox, G., 31, 133, 134, 135, 139, 145,
  149, 150, 166
Crossman, R., 138, 140, 166

Danziger, R., 160, 166
Davenport-Hines, R., 35, 167
Davies, M., 81, 167
democracy, 1, 2–3, 21–3, 29, 31, 38,
  45, 85, 156, 163–4
direct action, 2, 124
Doig, A., 73, 137, 167
Dowse, R., 85–6, 167
Dudley, G., 57, 167
Dunleavy, P., 152, 167

Eckstein, H., 36, 167
Economic and Social Committee, 95,
  104, 107
Edwards, R., 20, 167
Elbaum, B., 40, 167
Elliott, B., 17, 20, 21, 77, 85, 167
Energy, Department of, 57
Ennals, M., 13, 167
Environment, Department of, 57, 149,
  150
environmental groups, 2, 12, 59,
  80–1, 82, 88, 91–2, 106, 111,
  118, 127–8, 148–50, 159
European Commission, 61, 95, 102,
  104–6, 107, 108, 109

European Community, 64, 65,
  90–112, 135, 146, 154
European Council, 94
European Court of Justice, 91, 95, 97,
  98
European Parliament, 95, 104, 106–7

Farmers' Union of Wales, 17, 29
Farago, P., 48, 167
Field, F., 78, 81, 82, 167
Finer, S., 36, 167
Food and Drink Federation, 1, 54, 92,
  96–7
forestry, 140–5
Forestry Commission, 140–1
Friends of the Earth, 13, 14, 17, 19,
  53, 65, 77, 150, 159

Gilmour, I., 42, 43, 155, 167
government departments, 6, 30, 45,
  56–9, 129
government relations divisions, 6, 78,
  105, 107–8
Goyder, J., 12, 13, 14, 59, 80, 81,
  82, 86, 88, 118, 168
Greenpeace, 2, 13, 20, 77

Hall, P., 36, 168
Heclo, H., 31, 168
Hindell, K., 75, 168
Holmes, M., 33, 128, 168
House of Lords, 66, 70–1, 72
Howard League for Penal Reform, 15
Hughes, J., 85–6, 167
hunting, 75, 76, 77
Hurd, D., 162, 167

implementation of policy, 63–4, 91,
  109, 110, 130
insider groups, 14–21, 45, 56–7,
  65–6, 67, 80, 88–9
Institute of Economic Affairs, 50
Isaac-Henry, K., 20

Johansen, L., 122, 166
Jordan, G., 6, 12, 26, 30, 31, 32, 56,
  67, 168

King, R., 86, 168
Kirchner, E., 90, 168
Kogan, M., 79, 168

Labour Party, 1, 8, 76–7, 154

Lazonick, W., 40, 167, 168
Lively, J., 22, 168
lobbyists, 69–70, 73–4
local authority associations, 20, 22
local government, 85–9
London Food Commission, 52, 53, 54
Lowe, P., 12, 13, 14, 31, 59, 80, 81,
    82, 86, 88, 118, 134, 139, 141,
    148, 149, 166, 168
Lynn, L., 41, 168

MacDougall, D., 68, 168
McKeown, T., 41, 168
Marsh, D., 26, 34, 74, 75, 79, 89,
    168–9
mass media, 49–50, 54, 55, 79–84
May, T., 18–19, 169
Medhurst, K., 10, 11, 116, 169
Miller, C., 60, 63, 65, 66, 72, 126,
    169
Millward, F., 43, 165
Mitchell, M., 128, 169
Mitchison, A., 143, 169
Moe, T., 28, 169
Moran, M., 120, 122, 125, 169
Moyser, G., 10, 11, 116, 169

National Association for Freedom,
    84–5
National Consumer Council, 158
National Economic Development
    Council, 34, 43, 154
National Farmers' Union, 1, 8–9, 30,
    53, 55–6, 68, 87, 108, 120, 121,
    136–40, 146
National Federation of the Self-
    Employed, 17, 20
Nationalised Industry Chairmen's
    Group, 124
Nekkers, J., 41, 167
Nettl, J., 20, 169
Newby, H., 87, 169
Newton, K., 85, 169
Nugent, N., 18–19, 87, 169

Offe, C., 29, 132, 169
Olson, M., 27–8, 39–41, 156–7, 169
Oulès, F., 43, 169
outsider groups, 14–21, 55, 67, 87,
    88–9

Parliament, 57, 67–76
Paterson, W., 41, 57, 167

pensioner groups, 157
Plowden, W., 57, 169
pluralism, 25–30, 33
policy communities, 25, 27, 30–1,
    44–6, 56–7, 65, 91, 129, 138,
    140, 149, 159–60, 161
political parties, 2, 8–9, 30, 76–8,
    163
Porritt, J., 18, 76, 81, 83, 128, 129,
    159, 169
poverty lobby, 59, 122, 128–9, 132,
    161
pressure groups:
    definition of, 3–9
    primary groups, 9–10, 28, 86
    secondary groups, 9–10, 28
    strategies of, 14–21, 125–6
    theories of, 24–46
    typologies of, 11–21
    see also cause groups, insider
      groups, outsider groups, sectional
      groups
Presthus, R., 25, 117, 118, 169
private members' legislation, 74–6
Pross, A., 44–6, 169
protest groups, 2, 15
public opinion, 126–8, 163

quasi-governmental organisations, 6–8

ratepayer organisations, 15, 18, 87
Read, M., 74, 75, 84, 169
Resler, H., 30, 171
Retail Consortium, 123
Rhodes, R., 22, 169
Richardson, J., 6, 12, 16, 26, 30, 31,
    32, 56, 67, 169–70, 171
Roman Catholic Church, 116
Rose, R., 126–7, 170
Round Table, 103–4
Royal Society for the Protection of
    Birds (RSPB), 1, 13, 14, 144
Ryan, M., 15, 170

Salisbury, R., 22, 170
Sargent, J., 90, 96, 98, 112
Scharpf, F., 91, 94, 170
Schattschneider, E., 26, 170
Schmitter, P., 32, 33, 34, 35, 117,
    121, 170
Scottish National Party, 68, 78
Scottish Office, 137, 141, 145
secondary legislation, 63–4

sectional groups, 2, 5, 10, 12—14, 28, 50, 55, 73, 80, 83, 114—15, 118, 121, 124, 154, 155
Self, P., 9, 138, 170
Shanks, M., 158, 170
Simms, M., 75, 168
Smith, M., 120, 136, 170
social movements, 5—6
Society of Teachers Opposed to Physical Punishment (STOPP), 131—2
Solesbury, W., 50, 170
sponsorship divisions, 58—9
state, 21, 32, 33
Stedward, G., 5, 170
Stewart, J., 12, 170
Stewart, M., 86, 170
Stewart, P., 141, 142, 143, 145, 170
Stocker, T., 57, 107, 170
Stoker, G., 87, 88, 170
Storing, H., 9, 138, 170
Streeck, W., 41, 59, 117, 119, 121, 171
Stringer, J., 31, 171
Swaiger, K., 90, 168

Taylor, E., 63, 74, 171
technostructure, 44—6
Thatcher, M., 37, 39, 42, 43, 50, 129, 147, 153—4, see also Conservative Government, 1979—
Theakston, K., 58, 62, 63, 171
think tanks, 50
Thomas, R., 76, 124, 171

Tivey, L., 157, 171
Trade and Industry, Department of, 6, 33, 35, 58, 59
trade unions, 19, 29, 37, 38, 39, 42, 119—20, 124, 128, 154
Transport, Department of, 57
Truman, D., 26
TUC, 19, 26, 32, 34, 35, 128
Turner, A., 110, 171

van Waarden, F., 41, 168

Waldegrave, W., 129, 154—5, 171
Watkinson, Viscount, 80, 171
Westergaard, J., 30, 171
Whiteley, P., 20, 45, 57, 59, 60, 61, 78, 83, 84, 113, 116, 117, 118, 119, 121, 122, 125—6, 128—30, 157, 161, 162, 171
Whitston, C., 41, 57, 168
Wiesenthal, H., 29, 169
Wildavsky, A., 31, 168
Willis, D., 59, 171
Wilson, David, 89, 171
Wilson, Des, 155—6, 161—3, 171
Wilson, G., 138, 171
Winner, D., 18, 76, 81, 83, 128, 129, 159, 169
Winter, M., 31, 134, 149, 166, 168
Winyard, S., 20, 45, 57, 59, 60, 61, 78, 83, 84, 113, 116, 117, 118, 119, 121, 122, 125—6, 128—30, 157, 161, 162, 171